O9-AIG-207

This Is Earl Nightingale

This Is Earl Nightingale

by Earl Nightingale

Published in co-operation with
J. G. Ferguson Publishing Company
by Doubleday & Company, Inc.
Garden City, New York

Library of Congress Number 67–12840

Printed in the United States of America

For My Wife, Len

Foreword

Strange and wonderful things have happened to me with marvelous regularity for as long as I can remember. People and events of various sorts are forever coming along at exactly the right time to help me move from one interesting world to another. I had left broadcasting for good, I thought, in March of 1956. I remember vowing as I walked from the old familiar WGN studio in Chicago, "I'll never, as long as I live, sit in front of another microphone." (I had not, at that time, learned never to use the word "never.")

Earlier that same month I had written and

recorded a talk entitled "The Strangest Secret." I had done it on the advice of an acquaintance, never dreaming for an instant that I was setting in motion forces that were to sweep me into a new career of the most amazing kind. With absolutely no fanfare or advertising, strictly by word of mouth, that record began a movement that was to become an avalanche. Hundreds of thousands of copies of "The Strangest Secret" have been bought by people all over the free world. All by itself it began a new industry, and it continues to sell with undiminished volume to this day. And now its many brothers and sisters produced since that time are at work in many thousands of homes and in companies from the smallest to the very largest.

In the spring of 1959 another acquaintance suggested at lunch that I write and narrate a daily radio program for syndication. I told him of my vow regarding radio, studios, and microphones, and promptly forgot the matter. But later, during the summer, on a Canadian fishing trip with my son David, the memory of that conversation came to mind. And in the quiet, peaceful evenings in that beautiful setting I began writing the radio programs which we later called "Our Changing World." When I returned to Chicago, I recorded the programs I'd written and we sent them to a representative sampling of radio stations. Another avalanche!

In five years "Our Changing World" grew to become the largest syndicated radio program in the history of broadcasting. And it all started because of a chance remark and a Canadian fishing trip.

In this book we have tried to select from the radio broadcasts scripts which touch on a wide range of human interests. Their subjects range from Attitude, Conformity and Honesty to Using Time Wisely and the Law of Increase. We have tried to make of it a book which could be picked up at any time and opened at random, but which would, at the same time, be a carefully indexed volume for the writer, student, lecturer, or other person intent upon a definite subject.

Now, a word of thanks. My first thanks are due to the hundreds of radio stations and sponsors and to the millions of listeners who made these broadcasts possible; and to my partner, Lloyd Conant, and my other co-workers in Nightingale-Conant Corporation for helping make sure those stations, sponsors, and listeners got good service and good value for their money and time.

I'd also like to thank our creative director, John Graham, for his, I think, successful efforts to transform the copy I wrote for radio narration into readable prose (the two are quite different, as you probably know), and my good friend Betty Thanos for her work on the manuscript.

EARL NIGHTINGALE

Contents

Subject Index

This Is Earl Nightingale

1

The law of increase

How to Get Rich

Here are a few thoughts that you can make your own, thoughts which will guarantee you success all the years of your life. Now, that is quite a statement, but it's true.

To begin, let us understand that growth and increase are a part of mankind and all of nature. It is inherent in each of us to desire more. This is not wrong, it is perfectly natural, and the way it should be. This is true of all of us—the members of our families, our friends and associates, our customers. You should want to get rich in every department of your life. But what do I mean by "rich"? Getting rich, for you, is getting what you want very much. For some, it means a bigger income, or a large sum of capital. That is fine. You can get it without hurting, or even competing with, any other person. In fact, you can thereby increase the general well-being of everyone with whom you come in contact.

2 *The law of increase*

Unfortunately, the uninformed believe that you can only get ahead in the world at the expense of someone else. This is not true. No one can become rich in any way without enriching others. Anyone who adds to prosperity must prosper in turn.

Getting rich, for you, may mean obtaining more love, greater peace of mind, owning the home of your dreams, or accomplishing something else you've set your heart upon. In short, getting rich is getting whatever it is you want very much. It's as simple as that.

The first step is to understand completely that it is right for you to want what you want. All human activities are based on the desire for increase—people seeking more food, more clothes, more knowledge, more pleasure, more life.

The next step is to understand that you need not compete with or deprive anyone. Don't compete—create! In this way, you add to the general well-being without taking anything away from anyone.

Remember to give to every person more than you take from him. Now at first this may sound absurd, so let us dig into it a little. In order for a business or a person to expand—and remember, expansion is the natural desire of mankind—we must give more in use value than we charge. A building nail doesn't cost much, yet its use is great and goes on for years. This book didn't cost much; yet if you can get ideas from it that can bring you more than you now have, its use value will greatly exceed its cost.

How much does it cost to give love, respect, and consideration to those near you? Very little, just a little extra effort. Yet love, respect, and consideration are priceless to the person receiving them. This is the key: Give more than you receive in everything you do. In this way, you are building a great credit for yourself which must come to you in some form, sooner or later. You are taking out less than you are putting in, and by so doing you are building a tidal wave of future prosperity. This is the Law of Increase. It is understood and followed undeviatingly by every successful businessman, artist, professional man, and worker; by every successful mother and father and friend. It is the most striking attribute of all successful people, companies, or institutions.

Now, let us go back to creating instead of competing. You are the point from which all increase must stem. Not your company, your marriage partner, your parents, or your friends. You are the creative center of your universe. Increase must come from you personally. Find ways of doing the things you do which reflect you and your own unique talents and abilities. If you do this, no other person in the world can operate exactly as you do. You will not be competing with anyone, you will be creating from within yourself.

As you find new and better ways of giving more in use value than you are receiving in money, more and more people will turn to you. You will find your circle of friends increasing. If you are in business, you will find it continually growing, expanding. Do this in a quiet and unobtrusive manner. You don't have to shout about how much you are doing for others. If you are doing more for others, they will recognize it and be drawn to you.

One of the most interesting things about such increase is that totally unexpected and wonderful things will begin to occur in your life. People you don't know, who have exactly what you need, will make their appearance at the right time and the right place. Everything will begin to dovetail and your life will take on new meaning and direction and bring you far greater rewards. Let the impression of growth, of increase, mark everything you do.

As you do these things, keep constantly before you the vision of what it is you intend to accomplish. Don't worry about it; just know you are going to accomplish it and, following these rules, you cannot fail.

> *That man is truly free who desires what he is able to perform, and does what he desires.*
>
> ROUSSEAU

> *There are two things to aim at in life: first, to get what you want; and, after that, to enjoy it. Only the wisest of mankind achieve the second.*
>
> LOGAN PEARSALL SMITH

He is only bright that shines by himself.

GEORGE HERBERT

It is perfectly true, as philosophers say, that life must be understood backwards. But they forget the other proposition, that it must be lived forwards.

SØREN KIERKEGAARD

5 *The law of increase*

6

Learning

Our Changing World

Machines obsolesce because they are unable to change. Times change; they must and will, with ever accelerating momentum. As they do, the machines of today will be outdated. But human beings are not machines, however fond they are of acting like them; they can change.

Never before in the history of man has it been so necessary as it is today for us to develop a new awareness of ourselves with respect to our changing world. We need to face the fact that in the world of tomorrow, jobs will be radically different, many will be eliminated entirely. What can we do about it? We can take the advice of the former president of the University of Chicago, Robert M. Hutchins: "We can learn!" If we refuse to learn, if we insist on acting like machines, we may find ourselves idle tomorrow.

Every job is a part of a much larger organization. Organizations and industries don't die; they just change. The industry that once manufactured covered wagons is still here. But today it is making engines, tractors, and automobiles.

Let us say that through a set of circumstances a young man finds himself working as an attendant in a service station. He might wish he had done things differently, but it does no good to brood over the past. These are the facts: He is working in a service station. He wants to get married and have a home and children. And to do this, he decides that he must earn more money. His first inclination is to look around for a job that pays more. But before he moves to a different job, he should be aware that the move entails not only earning more but also learning a good deal more than he now knows. Otherwise, the chances are he will be no better off than he is pumping gas.

I think that instead of just looking at his job, he should look at the whole industry of which it is a part. In our example this is the petroleum industry, one of the world's largest and most profitable. Without leaving his job for the present, he could spend his free time studying the industry he is already in. Now, instead of being a service station attendant, he is a trainee in a major industry. He no longer has just a job, he has his foot on the first rung of what can be a fine and extremely rewarding career. By sticking with his studies and doing an outstanding job when he is working, he will soon be able to marry and have that home and, in time, anything else he wants. [Learning is the answer.]

The same thing applies to the boy working in the supermarket, the local factory, or as a salesman. Naturally, it is best to stay in school, for school is the best place to learn. But for those who have dropped out, the answer is the same. Learn! Learn all you can, and keep learning whether you are sixteen or sixty. And you will find your way—a way infinitely more interesting and substantially more rewarding—in this changing world of ours.

The minute a man stops learning, our world will begin to pass him by. He will be left a lonely and disconsolate figure in its wake. To learn or not to learn is a decision each of us must make.

The learning and knowledge that we have is at the most but little compared with that of which we are ignorant.

PLATO

If a man empties his purse into his head,
no one can take it away from him.
An investment in knowledge always pays
the best interest.

BENJAMIN FRANKLIN

Money

The Harvest of Production

Since the first coins were fashioned circa 700 B.C. somewhere in Asia Minor, money has been one of man's most interesting inventions.

But you might be surprised at the number of people who really don't understand just what money is, and why we get as much or as little as we do. One hears people say that money is not important. They're wrong! Money is just as important as the food it buys, the medical bills it pays, the education and homes it provides, and all the other things we cannot do without. It is absurd to say money is not as important as some other things. Nothing on earth will take the place of money in the areas in which it works.

And money is the harvest of our production. It is what we receive for our production, and what we can then use to buy the production of others. The amount of money a person receives will always be in direct proportion to the demand for what he does, his ability to do what he does, and the difficulty of replacing him. Of course this has nothing to do with the value of a human being as a human being. But most people can accurately measure the need for what they do, their ability to do it, and their indispensability by counting the money they receive for their work. Some exceptions to this rule of thumb may be teachers, research scientists, religious workers, and wives.

For example: A paper boy is just as important as a human being, as the president of the largest corporation. But since the paper boy can be replaced at any time, by virtually anyone, his income is small. On the other hand, the corporation president fills his position because of his skills and abilities, his knowledge, and as a result of many years of dedication and hard work. He therefore may earn as much in a month as another man earns in a year. A highly skilled brain surgeon can earn as much in an hour as an elevator operator might earn in a year. Our rewards in life will be in exact proportion to our contributions and the number of people to whom we contribute. Generally speaking, it can be said that if a person is not happy with the amount of money he is earning, he should examine his contribution.

A diamond is much more valuable than a lump of coal, but that is pretty much what a diamond was in the beginning. And, just as a diamond can be fashioned by nature from a piece of coal, a human being can enormously increase his value to the world. This is something, however, that each individual must do for himself.

A company growing at the rate of ten per cent a year will double in size in less than eight years. It might be a good idea to ask ourselves if we are growing in effectiveness at the rate of ten per cent a year. If we are, we should be able to double our income every eight years.

The use of money is all the advantage there is to having money.

BENJAMIN FRANKLIN

It's good to have money and the things that money can buy, but it's good, too, to check up once in a while and make sure that you have not lost the things that money can't buy.

GEORGE HORACE LORIMER

12

Creative thinking

Your Private Gold Mine

From time to time you hear somebody say, "You know, those people who got in on the ground floor of the opening of the West, with its gold and silver, really were fortunate. All that gold lying around, waiting to be baled and carried to market!" Or, you will hear: "And what about the early discoverers of our vast oil fields? All those derricks pumping millions of dollars' worth of black gold, and the folks who discovered it just sitting back and trying to keep their fortunes figured to the nearest million!" When I was a youngster during the depression, we used to sit around and dream of things like that. Maybe you've done the same thing.

Well there is one place that is virtually unexplored, where you can find all the wealth you'll ever need. Perhaps you never thought much about it, but each of us has his own private gold mine, all staked out, with a clear title, just waiting to be developed.

Try to get a mental picture of a gold mine (or an oil field) before it is discovered. No busy, noisy machinery, no crowds of men, no trucks and heavy equipment; just land covered with prairie grass and stretching as far as the eye can see to the distant horizon. Now, under that peaceful and innocent-looking piece of prairie is a wide, deep lake of oil, or a mother lode of gold worth millions. But you'd never know it was there, would you? Before the treasured oil gold was discovered, thousands of people must have ridden and walked right over it without realizing that right under their feet was a king's ransom, riches beyond their wildest dreams.

Somebody had to come along looking for it, someone had to be willing to risk digging for it. Somebody had to suspect it was there and start looking. His chances of hitting pay dirt with his first shovelful were pretty slim; but he believed that if he kept looking, kept digging, he would find it.

You and I have free title to the richest continent on earth. It is called the human mind, and it has produced just about everything you see and hear around you. It comes as standard equipment at birth, and maybe that is why most of us never use it; we don't value things we get free. Your mind has approximately twelve billion cells, and fully ninety per cent of it has never been explored.

The greatest thing on earth is a good idea. Consider the man who got the idea to dig under that prairie grass. Discovering a fortune was only the effect. His *idea* to dig was the cause. It was his *idea* that resulted in millions of dollars for him.

Now, how many ideas do you think you could get in a single day? Twenty, or thirty? Let us say you got twenty ideas a day. That would be one hundred a week if you didn't think on weekends. That would be fifty-two hundred ideas a year; fifty-two hundred holes you would be drilling. Remember—one idea can make you rich!

If you know anything about the law of averages, you will realize that before long you will have the idea you have been looking for. If the first ten, or first hundred, are no good, don't give up. The more dry holes, the closer you are to what you are looking for—your Big Idea, the one that will change your life!

Chances are that right now, as Russell Conwell used to say, you are standing in the middle of your own acre of diamonds. What you are looking for is the idea that is bigger than you are; one that will keep you challenged and interested for a long time to come.

The human race built most nobly when limitations were greatest and therefore when most was required of imagination in order to build at all. Limitations seem to have always been the best friends of architecture.

FRANK LLOYD WRIGHT

A great many people think they are thinking when they are really rearranging their prejudices and superstitions.

EDWARD R. MURROW

16

Opportunity

Greener Pastures

The other day I was reading about our universe and what we know and don't know about it—about the billions and billions of stars and planets, and of the millions of galaxies like our Milky Way, separated by voids so vast it takes light (which travels 186,000 miles per second) about two million years to cross these almost incomprehensible distances. There are astronomers today sitting in front of telescopes looking at stars, not as they are now, but as they were five hundred million years ago. That is how long it took the light from these stars to reach us, give or take a few years!

I have a hunch I know why astronomers and scientists are so curious, as we all are, about other worlds and other galaxies. It is partly because of what I call "greener pastures." The hope seems to spring eternal in all human beings that the opportunities are greater elsewhere. I suspect this uniquely human attribute, or frailty, has been at the root of all discovery.

[But it is a saddening fact that many people spend so much time thinking of other pastures that they never properly appraise their own.] While we are looking at what the other guy is doing and wishing we were in his pasture, others are wishing they were in ours. There is more opportunity hidden in our daily work than most of us could exploit in a lifetime. We need only look for it thoroughly enough, long enough to find it. It is like the story of the African farmer who sold his farm and spent the rest of his life hunting for diamonds the world over, only to have the richest diamond mine in the world discovered on the farm he had sold.

There is no such thing as a job that cannot, with time and thought, lead to greatness. But unless we spend the time, study, and effort to become outstanding at what we are now doing, why in the world should we think we could become great at something else? Somehow, succeeding always looks easier in the other fellow's line of work. It once looked so good to me that I too climbed the fence out of my pasture. By the time I had scrambled back in again, my little excursion had cost me thirty thousand dollars. I had gone into a business where I was short on experience and, as usually happens in such a case, I got burned on the wallet.

Now, I am not saying that you cannot go into a different business, but rather that you should first learn everything possible about it. And more important still, look long and carefully at the pasture you are now in. Chances are it is loaded with opportunities that someone else is going to profit by if you don't.

If you merely *compete* with everyone else in your line, you must be satisfied with the same returns, the same rewards, they are getting. But if you *create,* the sky is the limit. With the opportunities and experience you already have, you can build a stairway to just about anything you want.

Small opportunities are often
the beginnings of great enterprises.

DEMOSTHENES

It is not a question how much a man knows, but what use he makes of what he knows. Not a question of what he has acquired and how he has been trained, but of what he is and what he can do.

J. G. HOLLAND

A pessimist is one who makes difficulties
of his opportunities; an optimist makes
opportunities of his difficulties.

REGINALD B. MANSELL

Habit

The Magic Loom

We are all creatures of habit. We can do most things without even thinking about them; our bodies take charge and do them for us. When you dress, for instance, your mind can be completely preoccupied with something else. Your hands take over, independently, and do the whole job for you. All you do consciously is select what you are going to wear.

I can sit at my electric typewriter with my mind completely on the thoughts, words, and ideas I want to put down. As the ideas form in my mind, my fingers automatically spell out the words on the typewriter. In a way, it's uncanny. It is as though there are little subminds in each hand that translate the ideas into words, the words into letters, and then cause the right fingers to strike the right keys. Of course, the hands and fingers are not infallible, as any typist knows.

Habits, like people, come in all shapes and sizes. There once was a man who formed the compulsive habit of collecting magazines. He collected all kinds of magazines, thousands of them, which he carefully stored in great stacks in his attic. He did this for twelve years. One night he was awakened by a terrifying sound. The tons of magazines had finally reached the critical weight. The old beams gave a last agonizing cry, and then all his beloved magazines, along with the ceiling and the attic floor, came down on top of him in a final, fatal crash. He became another victim of what turned out to be a bad habit.

People are killed and injured every day as a result of bad habits. The person who forms the habit of smoking in bed may one day be immolated by it. Fatal or near-fatal ends also await the high-speed driver, the overeater, the overdrinker, the loudmouth, and the bully.

If you'll forgive a rather bad pun—we are indeed clothed by our habits. Just as a person such as a priest, a policeman, a horseman, or a house painter is known and recognized by the habit he wears, we are all of us known by the habits we form; good and bad.

A bad habit resisted is more easily resisted the next time. A good habit deliberately begun is more easily performed the next time. As the spider spins its web from delicate gossamer threads into a tough trap for the unwary, so we daily spin the threads of habit until they form themselves into cables, difficult if not impossible to break.

I had dinner once with a fine and very successful man who had somehow formed the habit of making loud, strangling sounds as he ate his soup. I was amazed and disappointed, as were the other diners within earshot. I said, "Your soup must be much better than mine." He asked, "Why?" And I said, "Because it sounds so much better." He just smiled and bent his head back to its noisy task. It was a habit I am certain he couldn't hear as we could.

As a parent, you may lay the foundation of poverty or riches, industry or idleness, good or evil, by the habits you instill in your children.

Habit is either the best of servants,
or the worst of masters.

EMMONS

What a curious phenomenon it is that you can get men to die for the liberty of the world who will not make the little sacrifice that is needed to free themselves from their own individual bondage.

BRUCE BARTON

It is easy to assume a habit; but when you try to cast it off, it will take skin and all.

H. W. SHAW

Self-knowledge

The Mysterious Trigger

Some of my friends and I were, on one occasion, talking in Des Moines, Iowa. One of us told a true story about a young man who quit school after a year in college and went to work as a real estate salesman. The young man was a complete flop in that field, and try as he would, he finally had to face up to the fact. He decided to go back to school. One night at a party he found himself in conversation with a student majoring in chemistry. As the chem major talked, our former real estate salesman found himself becoming tremendously interested. As a result of that evening, he signed up for the chemistry course even though he had never given a thought to a career in science. He was like a bird suddenly released from a cage: He went on to graduate with honors in chemistry and he has since made several notable contributions in that field.

I think this shows the importance of giving yourself a chance to discover what kind of work is right for you. [It makes you wonder how many frustrated, unhappy people there are; people who work at jobs they don't like—and who, as a result, are not successful—because they didn't find the trigger that would have fired their energy, ambition, and natural enthusiasm . . . the trigger to a lifetime career of interest, challenge, and rich reward.]

I believe that there is such a field for everyone. It could be any one of more than thirty thousand possible occupations, one of which is certain to be right for each of us. I suppose the problem is most people are not aware of the almost endless possibilities. Every young man in school should be on the alert for subjects in which he excels and finds interest, because every subject taught in school has within its broad circumference literally hundreds of fields in which a person can be happily and gainfully employed.

If the young real estate salesman had not gone back to school and gained a wider view, he might never have found his real place in the world of chemistry. Instead, he might have drifted all the years of his life from one unsatisfactory field of employment to another.

It is never too late to get into the work that is right for you. One of the happiest people I know went back to college at forty and is now fulfilling a lifetime ambition as a schoolteacher. And it's not necessary to go back to college. There are thousands of interesting and rewarding jobs that depend on interest and ability rather than educational qualifications. Half the battle is in knowing that somewhere there is a niche just right for you. You don't mind looking for something when you know for sure it's there.

Blessed is he who has found his work; let him ask no other blessedness. He has a work, a life purpose. Labor is life.

CARLYLE

Contentment

The Road to Peace of Mind

Experts in human psychology say you cannot change your whole personality. It represents a complex of too many long-established conditioned reflexes and behavior patterns . . . all those things that distinguish you as an individual.

But regardless of the personality you have (and it's probably better than you think), you can be content with yourself and your world. The way to achieve this peace of mind is to develop yourself as fully as possible. Each of us has a ceiling of performance. This ceiling is high in the areas in which you excel and low in the areas in which you have little or no aptitude. And your peace of mind or dissatisfaction is directly related to how far you develop your own abilities and aptitudes. If you knew how to use yourself fully—completely—you would know complete contentment. If you find yourself discontented, you should realize that it reflects your unfulfilled potential.

It might be a good idea to ask yourself just how much of your potential you think you are using. Would you say that you are operating at fifty per cent of your total potential? Thirty per cent . . . seventy-five per cent . . . ten per cent? Estimate the figure. A man who spends Saturday at home working on a new patio, or in the garden, is usually a much happier, more cheerful and contented man on Saturday night than the man who spends the day on the sofa. The person whose job makes him work close to his potential is a much happier person, as a rule, than the person doing a job that could be handled by a child, or a trained monkey. The tougher the job, the happier the person: this is only natural. Contentment comes to us when we become conscious of our powers and our abilities. The wife working on a new recipe that calls on all of her skills as a cook is too busy to be discontented or worried about herself and her ailments, real or imaginary.

It is important that each of us has a mental picture of the person he wants to become and that he tries day-by-day to come a little closer to fitting that picture. This gets rid of boredom and ennui, just as it gets rid of feelings of inferiority caused by working too far below our potential. And when you are dissatisfied, it is a good idea not to blame the work you do, but rather, the way you do it. Almost any job can offer a challenge if we attempt to do it superbly.

So if you find yourself discontented, examine the way in which you spend your days. The problem can usually be found there. Remember the great lines by Dean Briggs? "Do your work. Not just your work and no more, but a little more for the lavishing's sake. That little more which is worth all the rest. And if you doubt as you must; and if you suffer as you must—do your work. Put your heart into it and the sky will clear. And then out of your very doubt and suffering will be born the supreme joy of life."

Sometimes we seem to be concentrating so hard on reducing the work week that we forget the joys and satisfactions of life found only in our work.

Men are often capable of greater things than they perform. They are sent into the world with bills of credit, and seldom draw to their full extent.

WALPOLE

Conformity

Following the Followers

I remember reading an amusing story about a jeweler in a small town who noticed a man stopping each morning in front of his jewelry store, pulling a large gold watch out of his pocket, and setting it to the time of the large clock in the store window. He did this every day, month after month, year after year.

One morning, as the jeweler was sweeping the sidewalk in front of his store, the man in overalls stopped to set his watch. On impulse, the jeweler spoke to the man.

He said: "I've noticed you setting your watch by my big clock every morning for years. What do you do at the factory?"

The man finished winding his watch, replaced it in his pocket, and replied: "I'm the timekeeper. Every day at noon, my job is to blow the big whistle which tells everyone in town that it's noon and time to quit for lunch."

The jeweler hesitated for a moment, and then he said: "That's odd. I've been setting that big clock in the window every day, for all these years, by the noon whistle at the factory."

So it transpired that the people of this particular town had been quitting for lunch, and setting their clocks at what they thought was noon, but which was a long way from it.

Have you ever thought about the position we would be in if we spent our lives following the example of people who were in turn following us? It's a rather horrible thought, isn't it?

Although it's a perfectly natural tendency, this follow-the-leader game can get us into a lot of trouble and keep us from realizing our opportunities and our potentialities if we let it continue. Each of us should realize that what others do, the way others conduct themselves, is not necessarily what we should do, how we should behave.

We should form the habit of checking on things. If we hear some gossip, we should not believe it until we personally have proof that it is true.

I remember being told as a child that only poor people were happy, that rich people led miserable lives. Later, I could see this was a lot of nonsense. Some rich people are extremely happy and some who are poor are quite contented with their lot in life. Or, you'll hear some nonsense about a particular race or religious group. Don't believe it. Check on it. Beware, particularly, of generalizations. Start the habit of forming your own independent opinions through observation, study, and research.

If you believe what the majority tells you, you will be wrong most of the time for the one thing the great majority of people will fight hardest to keep, is their ignorance. Most people would rather appear absurd than admit they are wrong.

Enjoy your own life without comparing it with that of another.

CONDORCET

Insist on yourself; never imitate. Your own gift can present every moment with the cumulative force of a whole life's cultivation; but of the adopted talent of another you have only an extemporaneous half-possession.

EMERSON

Men are so constituted that everyone undertakes what he sees another successful in, whether he has aptitude for it or not.

GOETHE

Courage

The Phantom Wall

Have you ever stopped to think about how much more people could have, know, and do if they would only try? When timidity, self-consciousness, and vague memories of past failures all contrive to erect a phantom wall between us and the things we would like to have or do, we need courage to leap or painfully clamber over it and achieve our desires.

Emerson wrote: "What a new face courage puts on everything! A determined man, by his very attitude and the tone of his voice, puts a stop to defeat and begins to conquer."

Courage is often a matter of simple logic. Say a boy at a high school prom refrains from asking a girl to dance. He's afraid she might say "no," but he hasn't thought his problem through. By not asking her, he achieves the same result he would if he asked and she said, "no." The chances are excellent she is dying to have someone ask and that she's not too particular who does the asking. She wants to be seen dancing. But the boy refuses to risk success. The same can be true of success in later life. Men and women rule out the possibility of winning by refusing to risk defeat. They don't seem to realize that a lack of courage guarantees failure.

I remember a story about a man running toward a broad river. As he reached a dock he increased his speed, and when he came to the end of the dock, he threw himself as far out over the river as he could. He landed in the water about ten feet from the dock, swam back and climbed out. An amazed bystander asked him why he jumped into the river. He answered that a friend of his had bet him a thousand dollars to one that he could not jump across the river—and after a while he just couldn't stand thinking about those odds without at least trying.

Many things which look impossible from a distance become quite feasible once we muster the courage to make an attempt. There is always a way to reach everything desirable. If the man who tried to jump across the broad river had traveled upstream to its source, he would have found that he could step across it and win his bet.

Emerson said: "He has not learned the lesson of life who does not every day surmount a fear." And he gave a good reason for this when he said: "Fear always springs from ignorance." And again: "Men suffer all their life long under the foolish superstition that they can be cheated. But it is as impossible for a man to be cheated by anyone but himself as for a thing to be and not to be at the same time."

Yes, we cheat ourselves of the lives we could know, the things we could accomplish, the things we could have, because we're afraid to try, to ask. If we but knew ourselves better and the nature of the world, we would fear less and attempt much more.

Why not realize your ambition? If you really want it, if it is right, if it will not hurt another, then abandon yourself to it with the attitude and conviction of courage and it will be yours.

Courage consists, not in blindly overlooking danger but in seeing and conquering it.

RICHTER

Physical courage, which despises all danger, will make a man brave in one way; and moral courage, which despises all opinion, will make a man brave in another. The former would seem most necessary for the camp; the latter for the council; but to constitute a great man both are necessary.

COLTON

Security

On Becoming Indispensable

Have you ever heard a man or woman say, "Well, it may not be much of a job, but at least it represents security"? This way of looking at things is probably a hangover from the depression of the thirties. And it seems this word "security" has come to mean the wrong thing to most people.

In the first place, there probably is not a job in the world that offers security. If you have a job, any one of a hundred things could happen to cause you to lose it. But there *is* a form of real security anybody can develop, and once he has it, it can never be lost again.

If a man loses the one thing he believes represents security, he has lost everything. He finds himself suddenly in a cold and hostile world. He feels lost and doesn't know which way to turn. If you are old enough to remember the depression, you know what I mean. There were millions of people with vacant expressions on their faces wondering what hit them, queuing up in long lines at employment offices, waiting for a job to open up, any job, and in the meantime, chinning themselves on the relief rolls. The jobs these people had certainly did not represent security; they had folded early in the general economic slump.

All of us want a degree of safety for ourselves and our families in this changing world. If a job won't provide it, what will? Security is being an expert at what you do for a living. Security is being an uncommon person. Security is the greatness anyone can have if he will develop it. Security is never outside a person. If it isn't within, it isn't anywhere.

You have probably heard the expression, "You can't keep a good man down!" Well, you can't. You can take a good man and completely wipe him out, take everything but his mind and his spirit, and a wife who is willing to start over, and no matter where you put him, he will come bouncing right back. In a year, he will be back where he was when the ax fell. This man has the only real security a man can have. It is inside him, and his wife and kids can feel it when he sits down to the breakfast table; you can feel it when he enters a room, and you can see it in the way he walks and hear it in the way he talks. He is an expert at his business and he knows it. While most men are doing just as little as they can to get by, he is working and studying and planning and growing with his industry and his country. He does not feed on the economy, he contributes to it.

No matter what a person's job happens to be at this moment, it is loaded with opportunity—if he'll just look for it! If he will think about his work and constantly come up with ways to improve it, become better at it, in an almost unbelievably short time he will become practically indispensable. His company will start giving him more and more responsibility. When times are bad he will always be the last one to be laid off. And if that should happen to him, he can always find a place for the unusual skills and ability he has developed.

This is security, this and knowing enough to save at least ten per cent of your gross income, especially when times are good. Then, if something should happen to slow you down for a while, you are in a position to find the circumstances you want.

Circumstances! I make circumstances.

NAPOLEON

There's a man in the world who is never turned down, wherever he chances to stray; he gets the glad hand in the populous town, or out where the farmers make hay; he's greeted with pleasure on deserts of sand, and deep in the aisles of the woods; wherever he goes there's a welcoming hand—he's the man who delivers the goods.

WALT WHITMAN

There can be no security where there is fear.

FELIX FRANKFURTER

Problem solving

It Isn't the Job— It's You

Have you ever wondered why one person will make an outstanding success at the same job or business that another person will fail in?

While I was having lunch with an old friend, we got on this subject and it reminded him of a story about a distant relative. It seems this man found himself in Los Angeles right in the middle of the depression of the thirties. For some reason he decided to go into the real estate business. So he took care of the necessary preliminaries and opened a small office in Los Angeles on a street known as "Real Estate Row."

For a month this man sat in his office waiting for someone to come around to buy or sell some real estate. No one did. He began to notice that none of the other real estate offices were doing any business either; they were in fact, dying on the vine. It was the time of a widespread depression and no one was buying much of anything.

Three months passed while he tired to think of ways to keep from starving to death. One day he hit upon an idea. On the big Real Estate sign in front of his office, he printed down at the bottom in small, conservative letters these words: WE DO NOT HANDLE HOMES UNDER $25,000.

Almost immediately business began to come in. People who had homes valued at twenty-five thousand dollars and more began dropping in asking him to sell their homes. He called only on people who could afford twenty-five-thousand-dollar homes (and there were still quite a few around although they represented a microbic minority in those days) and he began to sell. He had restricted his business to the only people in the area who *could* buy and sell homes. And they, quite naturally, only wanted to do business with the real estate operator who catered to the kind of deals they were interested in. To make a long story short, he was very successful and actually became quite wealthy—even during the depression—in one of the hardest hit industries.

While real estate men all over town were crying on each other's shoulders about how terrible business was and how bad the times were, one man thought his way out of the dilemma.

Anyone, in any job or business, can do this. The very fact that you have a problem means there must be a solution. This isn't Pollyanna, this is good, sound, successful business and it's being demonstrated every day.

Some time ago I made a speech at the University of Georgia. The gentleman sitting next to me at the speakers' table told me we were in the heart of what has become the chicken-producing center of the country. He went on to say that some years back the area was deeply depressed until one man—one man—got the idea of giving eggs to farmers to incubate and raise chickens. All they had to buy was the feed, and he would sell their chickens for them. He made money, the farmers made money, and the entire area boomed. If there's a problem, there's a solution if you can just think of the idea for it and, as Red Motley says, "There's nothing in the world more powerful than an idea whose time has come."

No matter what we achieve—it consists of solving problems. But I think that we too often underestimate our own powers. You can solve problems just as well as the next person. Half the battle is *knowing* they can be solved.

> *Man is the favorite of nature, not in the sense that nature has done everything for him, but that she has given him the power of doing everything for himself.*
>
> ZACHARIAS

Imagination is more important than knowledge.

EINSTEIN

The four cornerstones of character on which the structure of this nation was built are: Initiative, Imagination, Individuality, and Independence.

CAPTAIN EDWARD V. RICKENBACKER

41
Problem solving

Achievement

Goal Achieving or Tension Relieving?

Here's an idea that intrigues me. See what you think of it.

Someone said, "Everything we do is either goal achieving or tension relieving." That's something to think about, isn't it? And use. If a man is not too happy with his progress in the world, he should take a good, long look at everything he does during the day and, as he approaches each act, he should ask himself, "Is this goal achieving or tension relieving?" We all need to relieve our tensions, but if we are doing too many things for escape and too few for achievement, we are going to hold ourselves back.

Wouldn't it be interesting if a survey could be made to discover how much time the average person devotes each day of the work week to acts which are strictly goal achieving. If this time could be subtracted from the sixteen waking hours typical for most of us, we might all be amazed to discover what a small amount of time we actually spend earning a living and preparing for the future. It would vary widely, of course, from industry to industry, and from job to job. The busy doctor, for example, might spend twelve hours a day actually in the presence of his patients. And every minute with a patient would have to be called "goal achieving."

Compare this with the way time is spent by a salesman. How much of his day is actually spent in positive acts? Driving from one call to another, even though he is not in the presence of a prospect or a customer, would have to be considered "goal achieving." But stopping for a cup of coffee would be tension relieving. So would chatting with people not in a position to buy his product, or reading fiction in a magazine while he is waiting to see someone.

There is a vital balance between tension relieving and goal achieving that each of us should give some thought to. Going overboard in the tension relieving department could lead to some serious problems in the future. Samuel Johnson once said, "Every man is, or hopes to be, an idler." There is, of course, a time to be idle and a time not to be idle. But if you want to be idle later, in comfort, it is a good idea to make sure you are not spending too much time in idleness now.

At any rate, I think it can be said that the success of a person in any undertaking will hinge directly upon his making certain that he relegates his tension relieving acts to a secondary position.

We carve out our own worlds in this life. The shape and size of them will be determined in large part by the balance we achieve.

Rest is the sweet sauce of labor.

PLUTARCH

A man who knows how to mix pleasures with business is never wholly possessed by either . . . and in the use of them he rather finds relaxation . . .

ST. EVREMOND

Absence of occupation is not rest; a mind quite vacant is a mind distressed.

COWPER

You never will be the person you can be if pressure, tension, and discipline are taken out of your life.

DR. JAMES G. BILKEY

Attitude

How's the World Treating You?

We live in a world of words. We have a word for everything, and some of these names and labels mean a great deal to us. Words such as "love," "happiness," "success," "achievement," "joy," and "ability" describe conditions all of us want. But there is one word which controls them all. That is, there is one word which describes a condition which will bring us all of these things, or keep us from getting any one of them.

If your youngster asked what this word is, could you tell him? If, from all of the many thousands of words in the language, you were asked to select the one which would influence your life more than any other, could you pick the right word?

[I call it the "magic word," and it is "ATTITUDE!"] Once we are grown and on our own, this word actually controls our environment, our entire world.

If you are curious about what kind of an attitude you have, a simple test will tell you what it has been up to this point in your life. Just answer this question with a "yes" or "no": "Do you feel the world is treating you well?" If your attitude toward the world is good, you will obtain good results. If your attitude is excellent, excellent will be your results. If your attitude is negative, little that is positive awaits you. And if your attitude is just so-so, you will live in a world that is not particularly bad, nor particularly good, just so-so.

Our environment, which is another way of saying how the world treats us, is nothing more than a reflection, a mirror actually, of our own attitudes.

One of the most pitiful aspects of society is the really large percentage of people who lead dismal, narrow, darkened lives, crying out against what appears to be a cruel world which they believe has singled them out for a lifetime of trouble, misery, and bad luck. Anyone who finds himself in such a prison of discontent should face the fact that he has very probably built his prison with his own hands. And unless such a person changes, his cell will continue to grow smaller and darker.

The world doesn't care whether we change

or not. Adopting a good, healthy attitude toward life doesn't affect life and the people with whom we come in contact nearly as much as it affects us. As it says in the Bible: "As ye sow, so shall ye reap."

It would be impossible even to estimate the number of jobs which have been lost, the number of promotions missed, the number of sales not made, the number of marriages ruined by poor attitudes. But you can number in the millions the jobs which are held but hated, the marriages which are tolerated but unhappy; all because of people who are waiting for others, or the world, to change toward them, instead of being big enough and wise enough to realize that we only get back what we put out.

In thirty days you can change your world and your environment by making this simple test. For thirty days treat every person you meet, without a single exception, as the most important person on earth. You will find that they will begin treating you the same way. You see, every person, as far as he is concerned, *is* the most important person on earth. How does the world look at you? Exactly as you look at the world.

'Tis a very good world we live in,
To spend, and to lend, and to give in;
But to beg, or to borrow, or ask for our own,
'Tis the very worst world that ever was known.

J. Bromfield

Youthfulness

When Your Dreams Die

How would you like a recipe for staying young? From earliest times men have believed that their search for a fountain of youth would be rewarded. They have sought it much as a man goes in search of happiness. And they have found that the secrets of both youth and happiness lie in the same place: within themselves.

A philosopher once wrote, "There is not much to do but bury a man when the last of his dreams is dead." That seems to be the answer—a person is as young as his dreams—for it explains why some people are old at forty, others still young at ninety.

Youth is a time for tackling new projects, and as long as a person is enthusiastically beginning something new, he will remain young in the only places that really count, in his mind and heart; he will be young in spirit. As Emerson said, "We need not count a man's years until he has nothing else to count."

The person who has no dream to spur him on, no goal to achieve, is already old; for age comes when hope and planning for the future die. This is why a man's lifework must be much larger than an eight hour a day job. Men only grow old in occupations with fixed limitations, uninteresting surroundings, and with no call upon the imagination or the mind. But some men stay young, regardless of their work. These are the men who are striving for something better, something greater. People who stay young are people who feel young, regardless of their years. They are people who like to try new things and who like working toward a goal whether they live long enough to reach it or not.

People who stay young never think much about old age or death. They concern themselves less with what might lie beyond the pale and more with the here and now, with today and tomorrow and next week. You'll never find them poring over the obituaries to see whom they have outlasted.

People who stay young keep their sense of humor; they know how to laugh, even when the joke happens to be on them. They do not hold grudges; if they are angered by something or someone, they are quick to forgive and forget. They seem to know that hatred hurts only the hater.

People who stay young look for and are quick to accept new ideas. They have a healthy curiosity about everything that comes within the range of their senses. They know that while they may slow down considerably from a physical standpoint, the mind can grow more able, more powerful with the years. A person can be at his best, mentally, at eighty or even older.

But above all, they continue in pursuit of a dream, something to earn or bring about, a new, higher plateau upon which to stand. Titian was painting masterpieces when he was ninety-eight.

What is the dream *you* are trying to bring into fulfillment? A person is as young as his dreams and as old as his doubts.

> *As I approve of a youth that has something of the old man in him, so I am no less pleased with an old man that has something of the youth. He that follows this rule may be old in body, but can never be so in mind.*
>
> CICERO

> *Few moments are more pleasing than those in which the mind is concerting measures for a new undertaking.*
>
> SAMUEL JOHNSON

Imagination

The Flywheel of Society

William James, in his Principles of Psychology, *defined genius as little more than the faculty of perceiving in an unhabitual way. In his essay on habit, he referred to habit as the flywheel of society; the thing that keeps us doing what we have been doing in the past; the thing that makes us fear change regardless of the present condition of our lives. And the genius, as defined by Dr. James, seems to be that rare bird who knows that change is not only good, but inevitable. He anticipates the inevitable. It is he perhaps who* makes *change inevitable. He habitually looks at everything about him in an unhabitual way. He takes nothing for granted. He knows that whatever he sees that is made by man, or served by man, is imperfect, is always in the state of evolving.*

Let me give you an example. A friend of mine was seeking a site for a large, luxury motel. He was in no hurry, and spent months in a large, West Coast city looking for the site that would probably best guarantee a good return on the considerable amount of money he was going to invest and borrow.

He found the perfect site. It was near a large university and at the intersection of five main roads, two of which were very heavily traveled. It was also within the city limits, which would mean a large local trade for the restaurant. There was only one hitch. On the site stood an old brick building housing a manufacturing concern which was still in business.

He called on the owners of the business and told them what he wanted to do. Since the city had, over the years, grown around the old building, he pointed out that it would be to their benefit to sell him the property at a price many times the land's original value and build themselves a new, modern plant in a less congested area. They saw the sense of his plan and a way to get nearly half a million dollars for their property. The deal was closed. He razed the building and built his motel.

Later, he discovered that many people in the motel business had looked upon that site as ideal for their purposes, but had written it off because it was already occupied. The point is that he saw it, not with the old brick manufactory on it, but instead with his beautiful new motel sitting there; he looked at that corner in an unhabitual way. And everybody benefited by his genius, including the community.

I think each of us can greatly increase the value of his life by taking to heart Dr. James's definition of genius; by looking at the things about us—in our home, and particularly in our work—with new eyes, with the eyes of creation. We can form the habit of seeing things, not as they are, but as they perhaps will be, as they could be, as our changing world insists they be.

Our lives are full of old brick buildings that we assume will remain standing where they are. And maybe they always will, if we don't do something about them.

Everything is in a state of metamorphosis.
Thou thyself art in everlasting change . . .
so is the whole universe.

MARCUS AURELIUS

There is nothing permanent except change.

WILL ROGERS

If you're still doing anything this year the same way you did it last year, you're behind the times.

ANONYMOUS

Goals

How to Get What You Want

I receive many letters from men and women all over the country who say they want to be successful, but don't know how. They have tried following all sorts of involved rules, yet they really need only one. Sir Isaac Newton was once asked how he discovered the law of gravitation; he replied, "By thinking about it all the time."

There is your answer—the only one you need: "By thinking about it all the time." Each of us becomes what he thinks about. This is what makes the millionaires, the bums, and all the people between these two extremes just what they are. So, if you can say what it is you spend most of your time thinking about, you can tell yourself what it is you are going to become. If that is not what you really want, you can change your destiny.

Consciously or—as is more commonly the case—unconsciously, each of us thus forges his own life and becomes great, good, average, fair, or poor. The late Mike Todd, the motion picture producer who made and lost millions, and then made them back again, was once asked if it didn't worry him to invest so much of his own money in a deal where he could lose it all. He answered to the effect that being broke is a temporary situation but poverty is a state of mind.

But just thinking and never doing will not help you get what you're looking for. Thought without action is as useless as action without thought. Let us say that a woman starts thinking about making a cake. She keeps thinking about it until she decides to get started. All that was necessary here was that she think about it with sufficient intensity to do something about it. There are many things to do in successfully baking a cake, so she does each of them in order, and that night she serves a cake to her family. But behind the reality of the cake is the thought.

The person who makes up his mind to reach a high and difficult goal must, in order to achieve it, do a great many things. But it is his constant thought that leads him to make it a reality. By looking at what any man past forty or fifty has accomplished, you can tell what he has spent most of his time thinking about.

Marshall Field, one of the world's most successful businessmen, had twelve rules for success, but none of them is worth much if a person does not know, and does not constantly think about, the goal he has decided to reach. Here are the twelve things Mr. Field would urge you to remember:

1. The value of time.
2. The success of perseverance.
3. The pleasure of working.
4. The dignity of simplicity.
5. The worth of character.
6. The power of kindness.
7. The influence of example.
8. The obligation of duty.
9. The wisdom of economy.
10. The virtue of patience.
11. The improvement of talent.
12. The joy of originating.

Your life is controlled by your thoughts. Your thoughts are controlled by your goals. Have you set your goals yet?

Thought in the mind hath made us.
What we are by thought was wrought and built.

JAMES ALLEN

We live in . . . thoughts, not breaths . . .
He most lives who thinks most.

PHILIP BAILEY

As he thinketh in his heart, so is he.

PROVERBS 23:7

58

Habit

The Rich Get Richer

People are often puzzled as to why a successful man continues to be successful, while unsuccessful people tend to remain unsuccessful. It is like the line in the song: "The rich get richer and the poor get poorer." This is really not true. The poor do not, as a rule, get poorer; but they do tend to remain poor, or at least at the bottom of the economic ladder, while the more successful and affluent tend to become even more successful.

I think the best reason for this is that we are all creatures of habit. People at the bottom of the economic scale are as bound by the habits that have resulted in their lack of financial success as the more successful people are bound by theirs. There is a conservatism of the very poor that is every bit as strong as the conservatism of the very rich. People, in general, tend to avoid anything that smacks of change. You would think the unsuccessful would welcome any kind of change, but they don't. They have grown used to their way of life and feel that change might be for the worse.

A successful person has set up a momentum like a heavy flywheel, and he keeps this momentum going through the habits that resulted in its getting started in the first place. Having formed good, productive habits and staying with them day in and day out, week in and week out, the successful person builds for himself an enormous, cumulative success factor; a kind of tidal wave that follows along behind him for perhaps three to five years, possibly even longer, but which eventually breaks over him with the force of accumulation.

On the other hand, the occasional good fortune that seems to come to the generally unsuccessful in a sporadic, hit-or-miss fashion is the result of their occasional productive acts which, unfortunately, they give up before they become established habits.

A good, effective act will always produce a good effect; but the effective acts must be maintained in a daily, habitual way if a person is to enjoy continual success and build the cumulative effect I spoke of.

The unsuccessful person has not really set anything genuinely productive going and kept it in motion. He will start something rolling, and then he will stop and watch while it slows down, loses its balance, and finally topples over. Success is like a rolling wheel with the only motive power coming from the person who starts it going. And in the beginning it is always more difficult to get this wheel started than it is to keep it going once it is set in motion.

Of course successful people run into setbacks and obstacles, too, but they tend to regard them as minor problems. They seem to know that if they will just stay with it, have faith in what they are doing and where they are going, sooner or later these problems will work themselves out. One of the least known factors about success is knowing how long it takes and understanding the importance of momentum—constant motion—and the formation of good habits.

Success in life is not so much a matter of talent or opportunity as it is of concentration and perseverance. As Sheridan said "The surest way not to fail is to determine to succeed."

> *We first make our habits, and then our habits make us.*
>
> DRYDEN

> *In most things success depends on knowing how long it takes to succeed.*
>
> MONTESQUIEU

When we have practiced good actions awhile they become easy; when they are easy we take pleasure in them; when they please us we do them frequently; and then, by frequency of act they grow into habit.

TILLOTSON

Friendship

Make New Friends as You Go

In replying to the tributes paid to him at a testimonial dinner, Herbert Bayard Swope once said, "I cannot give you the formula for success, but I can give you the formula for failure—try to please everybody."

One mistake made by most people is to believe you should keep all your friends, all your life. It cannot be done. It *should* not be done! H. L. Mencken said, "One of the most mawkish of human delusions is the notion that friendship should be lifelong. The fact is that a man of resilient mind outwears his friendships just as certainly as he outwears his love affairs and his politics. They become threadbare, and every act and attitude that they involve becomes an act of hypocrisy." As usual, Mencken put it bluntly; again as usual, he was right.

If you believe otherwise, you believe that a girl or boy should marry the first person she or he has a crush on. Or that we should still be going around with the group we went to school with. Mencken went on to say, "A prudent man, remembering that life is short, examines his friendships critically now and then. A few he retains, but the majority he tries to forget."

On the same subject, George Bernard Shaw wrote, "The only man who behaves sensibly is my tailor; he takes my measure anew each time he sees me, while all the rest go on with their old measurements and expect them to fit me." Living means changing, and changing means, or at least should mean, forming new friendships and discarding some of those we outwear. No two people mature at the same rate; some move ahead faster than others, and it is just ridiculous to try to retain all of our old friendships. Yet, people often feel guilty about outgrowing a friendship; they think they are becoming snobbish or being disloyal, when actually it is perfectly natural.

I do think that when we get older we form stronger and more lasting friendships than when we were young, changing, and moving around a lot. Our best and most lasting friends are those who think along the same lines, believe in the same things, and constantly challenge us to move ahead with them into increasing mental and emotional maturity. They are friends we enjoy spending an evening with, with a lot of good conversation over dinner and, maybe, far into the night.

Every time I spend a weekend with a certain friend of mine in St. Louis, or when he comes to visit me, we sit up until dawn discussing one thing or another. We disagree violently on several issues and it makes for really lively conversations. We may outgrow this friendship someday, but I know we will not until it is best for both of us to move ahead to other new and equally interesting associations. Having good old friends is wonderful but it is in some ways even better to look forward to the new ones.

It is not strange that even our loves should change with our fortunes.

SHAKESPEARE

Today is not yesterday. We ourselves change. How then can our works and thoughts if they are always to be the fittest continue always the same? Change indeed is painful yet ever needful, and if memory have its force and worth, so also has hope.

CARLYLE

Marriage

A Wife for 190 Pounds of Tobacco

Back in the year 1619, when the Colonists were trying to settle the stretch of beach now known as our Atlantic seaboard, a wife could be purchased for 190 pounds of tobacco. While it was as impossible then as it is now to place a value on a human being, particularly a female human being, in that time and place 190 pounds of tobacco was the going rate. That was the cost of transporting a woman from Europe to the Colonies, and wives were available.

Not too long ago a leading industrial psychologist said that a good wife can be worth a quarter of a million dollars in hard cash to her husband. This is in addition to bearing and raising his children, taking care of his home, and giving him the love and care he needs. I agree with this man wholeheartedly. There is just no way to determine the value of a woman who works with her husband and helps him reach the goals they have decided are important.

A friend of mine was having a difficult time with his business: it had been going steadily downhill despite everything he tried to do. Finally, after months of backbreaking work, worry, and lying awake nights, he realized he was going to have to tell his wife that he was almost broke. He asked her to sit down in the living room, and then told her the whole story. He was just about ready for the net by this time. When he had finished and felt that at last his world had come to an end, she went over to him, put her arms around him, and said, "We'll just start over again."

For a moment he sat there, stunned. Then it dawned on him that he *could* start over, and his mind began to review the mistakes he had made and could avoid the next time. Somehow, this had been the one thing he had never considered. He had been stewing for months, afraid to tell his wife about the condition of his business, afraid that she might think less of him. He should have known that most women are at their best when the chips are down. Women operate best when they are needed. The fact that this wife might have to move to a small apartment and give up the home she had grown to love was not nearly as important as letting her husband know that she was perfectly willing to go back and start at the beginning again. The way it worked out, they didn't have to sell their home. Although things were pretty rough for a while, he was a good man and a hard worker and pulled out in fine shape.

How can you place a value on a wife like his? If she had not been the kind of person she was, there is really no telling what that husband might have done, or the seriousness of the situation which might have developed. He promised himself never to keep her in the dark about the condition of his business again, because he realized that, when things were not going well, he could benefit from her strength and her ideas. Women are practical and have a way of thinking right to the middle of a problem. More men should talk over their jobs and business difficulties with their wives, and pay attention to their advice. Women often display an intuitive knowledge of just the right thing to do in a particular situation.

There is no question about it. A good wife can be the difference between a man's just drifting along or really accomplishing something.

All other goods by Fortune's hand are given,
A wife is the peculiar gift of heaven.

Pope

For nothing lovelier can be found

In woman, than to study household good,
And good works in her husband to promote.

Milton

Man cannot degrade woman without himself falling into degradation; he cannot elevate her without at the same time elevating himself.

ALEXANDER WALKER

Conversation

How to Avoid an Argument

Do you want to know how to avoid an argument? You can do it by the simple expedient of asking questions. Instead of jumping in and disagreeing before you know any more than the other party about the subject under discussion, ask that person to state his case specifically and define his terms.

People who will, at the drop of a hat, argue on any subject under the sun, are people who enjoy ruffling the feelings of others. Willis Sloane once wrote an article titled "Arguments Don't Win Friends," in which he pointed out that arguments are useless. They are more a matter of temper than temperate conversation and discussion.

I have found that an argument, like a potential highway accident, can generally be spotted from some distance away. And it can be avoided the same way: slow down and approach with caution. In conversation, as in driving, the worst danger is speed. It is pretty hard to get seriously hurt going ten miles an hour. You can avoid a serious dispute that could lead to a lot of heartache by just being extremely careful when you come upon a situation that is likely to erupt.

Subjects such as politics and religion can almost always provoke an argument. Racial prejudices, for example, can bring forth the most ridiculous statements for or against certain practices. But if you will apply this rule—make your opponent be specific—you may avoid a foolish argument.

If someone makes a statement that causes you to see sparks and feel the adrenalin pumping into your system, stop and ask, "Why do you say that?" If you get another absurd generalization, ask, "Would you mind being specific about that?" Ask questions such as "Why?" "How do you know?" Instead of trying to prove your opponent wrong, make him prove himself right. Put the burden of proof squarely where it belongs; then you can sit back calmly while he gets in over his head, flounders in the swamp for a while, and finally changes the subject. No argument. And he won't be so quick to start another one the next time.

Robert McNamara, when Secretary of Defense under Presidents Kennedy and Johnson, asked, "Why?" whenever something was proposed. Even if he was immediately against the proposal, he wanted all the facts. Perhaps he had been wrong about it; if he was right, he forced the person making the proposal to prove its merits.

No one can even guess at the number of families who live between arguments in a state of uneasy truce. It takes two or more to argue. Make certain you are not one of them. Instead, keep the pressure on the person who is a reckless-driver conversationalist, by asking what he means by what he says. Make sure you are going slowly with both hands on the wheel and one foot on the brake. It works wonders.

People who know what they want in this world are those who know how to achieve their ends without arguing. Arguments seldom make points, only enemies.

Strong and bitter words indicate a weak cause.

VICTOR HUGO

I never saw an instance of one of two disputants convincing the other by argument. I have seen many, on their getting warm, becoming rude, and shooting one another. Conviction is the effect of our own dispassionate reasoning, either in solitude, or weighing within ourselves, dispassionately, what we hear from others, standing uncommitted in arguments ourselves. It is one of the rules which, above all others, made Dr. Franklin the most amiable of men in society, "never to contradict anybody." If he was urged to announce an opinion, he did it rather by asking questions, as if for information or by suggesting doubts.

THOMAS JEFFERSON

Courtesy

It's Not Enough to Be Good

Riding on a bus the other morning, I was treated to a very interesting experience. The young driver drove expertly and as fast as traffic would allow. He was a good bus driver, but he didn't understand his job.

I sat right behind him, and all the way to my destination, I could see him failing as a person. Once, when stopped for a waiting passenger, we could both clearly see an elderly woman running as best she could to catch the bus. She was only three feet from the door when the driver closed it and drove away. Her tired, pained expression was a pitiful thing to see. Another time, a woman asked if she could get off at a particular street; he ignored her question, and I had to tell her that she could.

He knew how to drive a bus, but he had failed miserably in the human relations department. And his failure as a human being will always deprive him of a rewarding place in civilized society.

We encounter this sort of person far too frequently in our day-to-day lives. He is the person who does the technical side of his job thinking that is all he is paid to do, feeling no sympathy or consideration for others, closing his mind and eyes to the world of humanity that ebbs and flows about him.

As difficult as it may be, we should never get angry at such people. Pity them. Pity their ignorance, which keeps them existing at the bottom of the hole they have dug for themselves. Pity them for the miserable surroundings in which they must have been raised and educated; for the ignorance of the parents who failed, who somehow taught them hate and mistrust instead of love and compassion. Pity the wives or husbands who must put up with them, and the children who are being raised in such a bleak and barren environment.

Fortunately, they constitute a minority. They need to be taught the importance of treating people—all people, not just customers—with consideration and respect. If, after an attempt has been made to teach them, they still cannot learn and improve—if they still fail to see how a change in their attitude will help them as persons—they really should be fired. They need to find work, if there is such, where they don't come in contact with people. Let them wait for buses, not drive them; let them wait for good service, not withhold it.

Not long ago I was staying in a multimillion-dollar hotel in New York City that was doing everything it could to attract business, while down in the restaurant there was a waitress doing her level best, every day, to drive customers away. She had not been taught how to handle customers, and somebody in management was making a serious blunder in not training or firing her.

There is a certain percentage of the population that has never learned the lesson of getting on well with people. If you are in management you must learn to identify these people and either correct this fault or keep them out of your company.

The art of dealing harmoniously with others is one of the most important subjects you could choose to study. With it, there is no limit to happiness and abundance. Without it, there may just be nothing at all.

Nothing is more terrible than ignorance in action.

GOETHE

Nothing is so indicative of deepest culture as a tender consideration of the ignorant.

EMERSON

Nothing is ever lost by courtesy. It is the cheapest of the pleasures; costs nothing and conveys much. It pleases him who gives and him who receives, and thus, like mercy, is twice blessed.

ERASTUS WIMAN

Work

Keep Moving

Have you ever noticed that the longer you put off something you should do, the more difficult it is to get started?

Ironically, we deliberately add to the frustration and unhappiness we could so clearly avoid.

The great newspaper editor Arthur Brisbane once wrote: "Don't exaggerate your own importance, your own size, or your own miseries. You are an ant in a human anthill. Be a working ant, not a ridiculous insect pitying yourself."

Strong language, maybe, but it has a lot of sense for us. A person carrying a heavy weight is all right as long as he keeps going. The minute he stops, puts the weight on the ground, and sits down to rest, the weight seems to become heavier, the distance to be traveled greater, and the work just that much more unpleasant.

It can seem at times that things have piled up so high there's just no way of digging out—but there is. Pick the task that is most crucial and simply begin!

Just by plunging in you will feel better, and you will find that the water is not nearly as cold as you thought it would be. Keep at it, and before long the pile of things that seemed so overwhelming is behind you—finished.

It isn't the work itself that overwhelms us. It's thinking about how hard it is going to be. It's seeing it get larger every day. It's putting it off and hoping that somehow, through some miracle, it will disappear. The Chinese have a saying that a journey of a thousand miles begins with but a single step. And that step accomplishes two things. First, it shortens the distance we still have to travel. Secondly, and just as important, it instills hope; it strengthens our faith. If a person will just keep putting one foot in front of the other, he will be taken into new and exciting places and think thoughts that never would have come to him if he'd remained at the starting point. Then, when the journey is finished, he wonders how or why he could ever have sat so long and worried so much.

If you'll think back, you'll remember you have always been most contented after having finished a difficult piece of work or faced up to a responsibility you were worried about. It's never as bad as you think it's going to be, and the joy that will come with its accomplishment makes it more than worth while. Work never killed anyone. It's worry that does the damage, and the worry would disappear if we would just settle down and do the work.

An American president said: "All growth depends upon activity. There is no development physically or intellectually without effort, and effort means work. Work is not a curse; it is the prerogative of intelligence, the only means to manhood and the measure of civilization."

And it never hurts to do a little something extra just for the lavishing's sake. Elbert Hubbard put it this way: "People who never do any more than they're paid to do are never paid for any more than they do." Payment comes in many forms, but always in exact proportion to what we do.

Heaven never helps the man who will not act.

SOPHOCLES

By the streets of "by and by" one arrives at the house of "never."

CERVANTES

Our grand business is not to see what lies dimly at a distance but to do what lies clearly at hand.

CARLYLE

Children

That's What They're Trying to Do

I remember hearing an angry father shout at his twelve-year-old son, "Why don't you grow up?" There was a sudden silence in the room, and then the boy, his face working to control his tears, quietly said, "That's what I'm trying to do."

That's presumably what all young people are trying to do and it's not an easy job. As adults, we tend to be impatient with others who cannot do as well, as quickly, something that took us perhaps years to learn—if, indeed, we have completely learned it ourselves.

To the skillful, the fumbling, awkward attempts of the novice often seem ludicrous, or exasperating, if not totally incomprehensible. "No, no," we say, "that's not the way to do it!" And in we charge to take over. In doing so, we add humiliation and self-consciousness to the beginner's feelings of inadequacy.

When we humiliate anyone by treating him as though he were an inept, bungling fool, he will begin to hate us. And each time we jump on him again—each time we tell him how inadequate he is with such remarks as "Won't you ever learn?" or "You're impossible" or "You can't do anything right" or "Why don't you grow up?"—we feed a little additional fuel to the fire.

If someone talked to us that way, we'd punch him in the nose, but youngsters can't do that, much as they'd love to. The fire just builds within them. They react to the parent who treats them thusly just as you or I would. They're terribly disappointed in the parent and in themselves. They're torn by the wish to love, the need to love, and the hate they feel. This is the kind of tumultuous inner battle that an adult finds most difficult to handle and resolve. In a child, or a very young person, when everything in life looms so much bigger, so much more final and terrible, it takes on catastrophic proportions.

Later, when the young person has grown into adulthood and, hopefully, some degree of maturity, he and his parent, or parents, may become friends again. He may even make exactly the same mistakes with his kids.

It's a costly shame that we use a double standard in dealing with our children and with other people. Not all parents do; some parents treat their youngsters with courtesy, respect, and love and, at the same time, lay down firm guidelines and rules of conduct.

Being a good parent must surely be one of the world's most difficult jobs, exceeded in difficulty only by the process of growing up itself. It's a job for which most of us had no training, and little more than the resolution to try to do a better job than our parents did with us. But if there's a key word to successful child rearing, I rather imagine it's the same word which is the cornerstone of successful marriage: courtesy. It's showing those we love and for whom we are responsible the common courtesy and respect we show to total strangers.

Living in close and constant proximity makes this difficult, perhaps, but no less necessary.

When it comes to raising children, everyone thinks he's an expert, and I guess I'm no exception. But if we tried to follow the advice of all the so-called experts in this field, nothing we did would be right. Except, maybe, using a little courtesy.

The wildest colts make the best horses.

PLUTARCH

The best way to make children good is to make them happy.

WILDE

The sacred books of the ancient Persians say, if you would be holy, instruct your children, because all the good acts they perform will be imputed to you.

MONTESQUIEU

Service

Who's Your Boss?

I'll bet you could ask a thousand working people the question "Who's your boss?" and never get the right answer.

There is only one boss, and whether a person shines shoes for a living or heads the largest corporation in the world, his boss remains the same. It is the customer. Here is the one person who pays everyone's salary and who decides whether a business is going to succeed or fail. He doesn't care if a business has been around a hundred years. The minute it starts treating him badly, he'll put it *out* of business.

This boss, the customer, is actually the one who buys everything you have or will ever own. He has bought all of your clothes, your car, your home, pays for your children's education and your vacations. He pays all of your bills, and he pays them in exact proportion to the way you treat him.

The man who works deep inside a big plant on an assembly line might think he is working for the company that writes his paycheck, but he is not. He is working for the person who buys the product which comes off the end of the line. If the person doesn't like the product, he will not buy it, and eventually, if this continues, in effect he fires the man on the assembly line. In fact, he will fire everyone in the company from the president on down. He can do it by simply spending his money for some other product. This is one of the reasons why taking pride in the work we do is so important to us personally. Aside from the joy that comes from doing an exceptionally good job, it will help get more customers, keep the ones we have, and ensure the weekly paycheck.

I once patronized a laundry that kept breaking buttons on my shirts. I no longer send the shirts to them. There must be hundreds of men who have had the same experience with this particular laundry. Eventually—it may have already happened—the person running the press, who kept breaking the buttons, has to lose that job. The customer loses, the company loses, the employee loses. This doesn't help anyone.

Some companies that had large, flourishing businesses a few years ago are no longer in existence. They couldn't, or didn't, satisfy the customer; they forgot who the boss really is. Some brand names that once were famous, that were leaders in their fields not so long ago, have disappeared; others are bigger and better than ever. The customer is always fair. He can be won back, if you don't let him go too long. He will spend his money with you if you earn it, and he will bring his friends.

You can get in your car and drive across the country and tell by looking at any business, from a little corner grocery store to a mammoth corporation, exactly how it is treating the boss, by seeing the way the boss has been treating the business.

Knowing who the boss really is and how to treat him can make all the difference—not only between success and failure, but also between happiness and frustration.

The vocation of every man and woman is to serve other people.

TOLSTOI

Right or wrong, the customer is always right.

MARSHALL FIELD

Nothing in this world is so good as usefulness. It binds your fellow creatures to you and you to them. It tends to the improvement of your own character and gives you a real importance in society much beyond what any artificial station can bestow.

B. C. BRODIE

Conformity

The Danger of Laughter

Do you know what form of punishment people dread more than any other? It is laughter. As a wise man once wrote: "The deepest principle of human nature is the craving to be appreciated." And the exact opposite of being appreciated is to be laughed at. In fact, among the Eskimos, laughter is the only punishment for thieves. If a person is found to be a thief, all the Eskimos in the village laugh at him whenever they see him. As a result, there is very little stealing among Eskimos.

This is the reason youngsters in school want to dress alike. I drove by a corner the other day where four or five girls of high school age were waiting for a school bus. They were all wearing identical coats. It appeared at first that they belonged to some kind of uniformed organization. Even though dressing alike had the effect of removing their individuality and causing them to blend in with the crowd, it apparently was much better in their minds than running the risk of being laughed at. And since a child will laugh more quickly than an adult at an individual who is different, children are much more conscious of wearing something different from what all the other kids are wearing.

Laughter can be the severest form of criticism, and the fear of criticism keeps us from doing a lot of things. It keeps us from doing some things we should not do, as laughter keeps Eskimos from stealing, and that is good; but it also keeps us from doing a lot of things we might be better off doing.

It can be one of the enormous pressures of environment. Take, for example, the worker who avoids doing an outstanding and conscientious job because of the fear that his more cynical associates might laugh at him. Here, the fear of criticism in the form of laughter could misshape a man's life. It could keep him from the goals and achievements he might reach if he weren't so conscious of how his actions would appear to others. It is here that a better understanding of what is right and wrong can overcome a person's fear of criticism. F. D. Huntington wrote, "Conduct is the great profession. Behavior is the perpetual revealing of us. What a man does, tells us what he is."

Frequently, being right and doing what is right can bring down upon us criticism and derision, while going along with things, even though we know they are wrong, will keep us "in good" with the crowd. And it is at this point that the men are separated from the boys. When our desire to belong to our crowd is more important to us than standing up for what we know to be right we ought to examine our resources. We may just be lacking two of the most important attributes of a human being, courage and maturity.

Winston Churchill once said, "Courage is the finest of human qualities because it guarantees all the others." Certainly, if there is one vital aspect of living successfully that we should get across to our youngsters, this is it.

If our kids want to dress like all the others in class, fine, it's normal. We were the same way when we were their age. They should be told, nevertheless, *why* this is important to them: that the desire to belong, to be liked, is natural. But they should also be told that it should come to an end one day—that in true maturity we grow into individuals with individual thinking, individual goals, individual action; that we will be happier if we do our work and live our lives as best we possibly can, even though it may be the fashion among others to slide along as easily as possible.

Ridicule is frequently employed with more power and success than severity.

HORACE

Whoso would be a man must be a non-conformist.

EMERSON

The virtues of the strong man are like the wind. The virtues of the common man are like the grass. The grass, when the wind passes over it, bends.

THOREAU

91
Con-formity

Conversation

The Art of Listening

Bennett Cerf tells of a college professor, much admired in his field, who would often invite his more promising students to his home for informal get-togethers. On one such occasion an eager sophomore asked: "Professor, what's the secret of the art of good conversation?" The professor held up an admonishing finger and said, "Listen." After a long minute had passed, the sophomore said, "Well, I'm listening." And the professor said, "That—is the secret."

It is also something that we would do well to check ourselves on from time to time. What brought this to mind was a luncheon I recently suffered through in the company of a person who obviously had never taken the time to learn the secret of the art of conversation. I am sure you know the type. He can be recognized by his rapidly moving mouth from which issues little or nothing of value. He seems to feel there is something wrong with silence and reflection.

Someone else has said that good conversation is like a tennis match in which the subject of conversation is lobbed back and forth, with everyone participating. But with those who have not learned this valuable art, you are more like a spectator at a golf match, simply standing by while some fellow keeps hitting his own ball.

These are times when you would like to have a tape recorder and a hidden microphone so you could send the conversation-dominator a recording of his one-way diatribe. Then he could hear himself riding roughshod over others, curtly dismissing their comments, and churning back into his own stream of sound like a hippopotamus in a millpond.

Listening really is the key to good conversation. You can't learn much with your own mouth open. Whatever you say has to be something you already know . . . unless you are guessing or, worse still, faking, in which case you are riding for an embarrassing fall.

The most embarrassing moments I can recall have been the times I was talking when I should have been listening. So every once in a while, I remind myself to be a good listener. Then, when it is my turn to add something to the general conversation, perhaps I can add something of value or interest.

It's not an easy thing to do. Especially when the conversation turns to a subject on which you have a strong opinion. There is a great temptation to jump in with both feet, flailing arms and working jaw, submerging the entire room in one's own great wisdom. But if one will summon the self-control and resist the urge, one can then parcel out his familiarity with the subject in small amounts. This permits others to share the topic. A person just might, through this method, manage to sound relatively intelligent all evening.

And if you run across a conversation hog, don't try to compete. If he runs down, which isn't likely, toss him another subject. You will find he is an expert on everything under the sun, and while he is talking, you can be thinking constructively of something else.

> *The great charm of conversation consists less in the display of one's own wit and intelligence than in the power to draw forth the resources of others.*
>
> BRUYÈRE

It is good to rub and polish our brain against that of others.

MONTAIGNE

You must originate, and you must sympathize; you must possess, at the same time, the habit of communicating and the habit of listening.

LORD BEACONSFIELD

Integrity

A Word to Live By

When General Dean was a prisoner of the Communist Chinese in Korea and had been led to believe that he would soon be shot, he wrote a letter to his wife with instructions for their son. He wrote: "Tell Bill the word is integrity."

Here is the best advice a parent can give to a child. With that single word and realizing all that it means, a young man or woman can look forward to a tremendously rewarding life. It will mean living by the Golden Rule, an insurance policy that guarantees abundance.

Integrity is the quality we most often look for in others. It is what a woman wants in her husband, and he in her. It is what the boss wants of his employees, and vice versa. If you are having a home built, it is what you want most from the men who work on it whether you are there to watch them or not. Integrity is the world's most valuable quality in a service, a product, or a person.

If one uses the word "integrity" as a guide for all his dealings with others, he can rest easy in the knowledge that he will find it coming back to him in countless ways. One of the greatest rewards is the feeling of personal worth and the confidence and assurance integrity brings.

The man or woman of integrity doesn't have to contend with a haunted house full of fears and worries. Since this person treats everyone with whom he comes in contact and everything he does with integrity, it will be reflected throughout his world.

There are probably millions of people who would not steal someone else's property but who think it is all right to give less than their best to their work. They don't think of this as stealing, but it is. What would you consider it, if such a person were working to build your home? Frequently our attitude changes with the situation. An incompetent waitress, out to dinner with her boyfriend, will be the first to complain about poor service. A sloppy builder will suspect a sloppy attitude toward something being built for him, and he will yell his head off if he finds it.

We look for our own shortcomings in others. But the man or woman of integrity, expects integrity in others as a matter of course.

Over the long haul, the person who lacks integrity in any aspect of his life—at work, at home, or with his social contacts—is a person who has failed to mature. He lacks wisdom, and he will suffer for it. Seldom does this type of individual ever wake up to the fact that he is simply sawing off the limb he is sitting on, and sooner or later he has to take his fall.

General Dean, undoubtedly, gave a lot of thought to the advice he wanted to leave his son. If he had thought for ten years, he could not have come up with a better word than integrity.

I am a true laborer;
　　I earn that I eat,
Get that I wear;
　　Owe no man hate,
Envy no man's happiness,
　　Glad of other man's good.

Shakespeare

Integrity is the first step to
true greatness.

C. SIMMONS

Nothing more completely baffles one
who is full of tricks and duplicity
than straightforward simple integrity
in another.

COLTON

Truth

The Most Important Thing

Do you think people are ignorant because they are poor, or poor because they are ignorant? I personally believe that the latter is true and have formulated a rather special definition of the word "poor."

Ask yourself: "What's the most important thing on earth as far as a human being is concerned?" I think it is *truth*. Truth is knowledge, and truth is honesty. To the extent that a person has knowledge, and personal honesty, he is rich.

Mirabeau once said: "If honesty did not exist, we ought to invent it as the best means of getting rich." Shakespeare wrote: "To be honest as the world goes, is to be one man picked out of ten thousand." Both of them were right.

To be ignorant is to be poor. It does not have to do with money, necessarily, although one seldom finds a person with knowledge who is not getting along well in the world. He may not be wealthy in the conventional sense, but he has enough for his needs, and he's enormously wealthy in many important ways.

A person will enjoy life, the world, and people to the extent that he moves away from ignorance and toward knowledge. Perhaps just as important, or even more so, the degree to which a person has truth and knowledge will determine his degree of freedom as an individual. Every human being has to be born ignorant and, for a time, live in ignorance. But if he remains ignorant that is his own fault. The fight against ignorance waged by everyone during his or her lifetime must be an individual, personal thing. No one can give us truth. Another person can point out the truth and urge us to strive to make it our own, but it is far too great a thing to be received passively. It must be searched for actively if it is to have significance. We can be inspired to search for truth, but unless we find it for ourselves it will do us little good.

A strong man cannot make a weak man strong. But a weak man can make himself strong by following a planned course of action for a given time and, of course, a strong man can make himself stronger.

To my way of thinking, each of us has the opportunity for freedom and the wealth that comes with knowledge and understanding. If we decide to stop before we have reached our riches, we should blame no one but ourselves.

I believe a man is poor to the extent that he is ignorant because the riches and the freedom he seeks—if he is truly seeking them—are all around him. They are under his feet and perched on his shoulder, they are in the public library and the corner bookstore. Truth and the riches it brings surround us every day of our lives. If we do not see them, we are poor indeed.

Horace Mann put it this way: "Keep one thing forever in view—the truth; and if you do this, though it may seem to lead you away from the opinions of men, it will assuredly conduct you to the throne of God."

The spirit of truth and the spirit of freedom—they are the pillars of society.

IBSEN

We are born to inquire after truth.

MONTAIGNE

The greatest homage we can pay to truth is to use it.

EMERSON

To restore a commonplace truth to its first uncommon lustre you need only translate it into action.

COLERIDGE

Self-confidence

The Belief Button

The other night over dinner I was talking to good friend of mine who is a hypnotist, about hypnosis and some of the amazing things that can be done with it. My friend pointed out that what hypnosis does is simply obtain a clear shot at a person's belief *button. That is, a person hypnotized by someone who knows his business, gets rid of all doubts and believes almost everything he is told. He will not believe or do anything that he cannot believe, but there is a wide area of belief that can be reached.*

Once a person believes he can do something, he *can* actually do it. That is why painless operations are possible under hypnosis—why even bleeding can be controlled. A hypnotized person can do amazing things that he would never do in a waking state. But a person can do nothing under hypnosis that he could not do in his waking state, if he only believed he could. We are not given new strength when we are hypnotized; strengths we already have are simply brought out.

We are, however, so full of doubts; we are so suspicious of our own abilities under normal circumstances that we operate far below our capabilities.

Here is but one example. A salesman had been employed by a major concern for seven years. During those seven years his commissions had averaged $7700 a year, a reasonable income—the kind of income a fairly hard-working salesman could expect to make. One day this salesman got the idea that he was not operating as efficiently as he could. He was sort of coasting along, doing a pretty average job because that was what the other fellows were doing. He was earning more than some and less than others; he was accepted and he was getting along.

He was not hypnotized, but because he received some inspiration to do better, he began really utilizing his time and ability. The first year following this decision he almost tripled his income to more than $22,000. He added a swimming pool to his home, bought a new car, and took a trip to Europe all in that same year.

This is a true story, and I have a letter to prove it. He had previously "hypnotized" himself into believing he was an average person (actually there is no such thing) and had performed in accordance with what he believed himself to be. As soon as his belief changed, as soon as he envisaged himself doing three times as well, he began to act this new part and everything fell into place.

Today he is living a far more successful, interesting, and exciting life. He and his wife are enjoying all the things they used to dream about. This is not self-hypnosis, it is merely understanding that the picture we habitually hold of ourselves is far smaller than it could be. We know we could do amazing things under hypnosis simply because we would believe we could. Why not maintain this belief in our waking state? This is what Socrates was talking about when he said, "Know thyself."

Most of us normally perform far below our capabilities simply because we lack faith in ourselves. This can be changed. The great line appears in Mark 9:23: "If thou canst believe, all things are possible to him that believeth."

In actual life every great enterprise begins with and takes its first forward step in faith.

SCHLEGEL

Self approbation when found in truth and a good

conscience is a source of some of the purest joys known to man.

SIMMONS

Confidence imparts a wondrous inspiration to its possessor. It bears him on in security, either to meet no danger or to find it a matter of glorious trial.

ANONYMOUS

106

Motivation

How Much Can You Do?

We have all read news stories from time to time telling of almost superhuman feats performed by people under the pressure of strong emotional stimuli.

A twelve-year-old boy lifted, off the legs of his father, a log so heavy that four men could hardly budge it later. A slender housewife, whose husband had been pinned beneath the car he was working on when it slipped off the jack, succeeded in raising one end of the car sufficiently for him to wriggle out. Seeing a truck driver trapped in the crushed and burning cab of his wrecked truck, a man crawled in through the window and, bracing his feet, put his back against the smashed top and raised it enough for rescuers to remove the driver.

During a bombing attack in World War II, I saw a sailor jump from a platform high on the mast of a battleship and land on a steel turret far below without even spraining his ankle. Under normal conditions, he would have been killed or at least have broken the bones in his legs and hips.

The point I want to make is that we don't even know what our potential is, until we are moved by some strong stimulus.

I think this is why people who are in work they hate often do such a poor job, and why people who are in work they love do so well. People with a burning desire to accomplish some ambitious goal do accomplish it; while others, without a powerful emotional impetus behind their actions, will fail at the same thing.

This goes a long way toward explaining why some of the least likely people become such outstanding successes. This is why the homely girl becomes a leading actress; or the boy with the terribly burned legs becomes a world's champion track star; or the quiet, chubby kid in school goes on to make millions and carve a name for himself in industry and finance. On the other hand, Hollywood is full of beautiful women and handsome men who will never reach stardom because they lack the most vital ingredient of all: the will . . . the great craving to succeed.

The people who go on to great success in the world do not accomplish their goals because they know somebody, or have cheated somebody, or stepped on a competitor, or "got the breaks;" I don't care what the cynics say. I have studied too many of these cases to be fooled. These people get to the top because they have to; because inside them burns a dream too big, too ever-present, too demanding to be denied.

That is why it is foolish to suggest that they settle for less, or that they are wrong in their drive for greatness. It is not that they just *want* to get to the top; they *have* to, and there's nothing in the world they can do about it. They would be miserable in any other kind of existence. They accomplish the seemingly impossible because of a great need—an emotional stimulus that forces them over every obstacle—that makes them begin again no matter how many failures they encounter along the way. They succeed simply because they insist on it.

> *Few things are impracticable in themselves, and it is for want of application rather than of means, that men fail of success.*
>
> ROCHEFOUCAULD

> *We can do anything we want to do if we stick to it long enough.*
>
> HELEN KELLER

The greatest single thing in the qualification of a great player, a great team, or a great man, is a desire to reach the objective that admits of no interference anywhere.

BRANCH RICKEY

Saving money

You'll Be Glad and Sorry

There is an old fable about a man who was riding across the desert at night. As he was crossing a dry river bed, a voice came out of the darkness ordering him to halt. The voice then said, "Now get off your camel."
The man got off, and the voice said, "Pick up some gravel from the river bed." The man did. Then the voice said, "Now mount and ride on. In the morning you'll be both glad and sorry."

When it became light enough, the rider looked at what he had picked up from the river bed and discovered it was not gravel at all—it was a handful of precious gems! And, as the voice had said, he was both glad and sorry. Glad he had picked up a few, and sorry he had not picked up more. Like most fables, this one is based on human nature, and I guess it is particularly true right here in America.

I think we all realize that we are living in the richest country the world has ever known. As a matter of fact, we are right in the middle of the Golden Age man has dreamed of since the days of Pythagoras, Plato, and Aristotle.

The American worker, compared with those in most countries (particularly those on the shady side of the Iron Curtain), is a wealthy man. Compare his income and his standard of living to Americans of fifty years ago and he is a regular tycoon!

But most modern American families are like the man in the fable who picked up the few precious stones thinking they were gravel. They are glad they have such a high standard of living, but about ninety-five per cent of them wind up sorry. Sorry because they never woke up to the fact that financial independence has nothing at all to do with the money you are paid but only with the money you *save!*

Imagine one hundred young American men who all start even at age twenty-five. Forty years later, when they are sixty-five, only one out of the original one hundred is well-to-do; four are financially independent for life; the rest, the ninety-five per cent, didn't make it. This would not sound so bad perhaps in some famine-ridden, under-nourished, and depressed country. But this terrible situation is going on right here.

It is a little known fact that regardless of what a man happens to do for a living, he can be financially independent for life by the time he is sixty-five if he will only give a dime out of every dollar to the forgotten man—himself—and the forgotten family—his own.

The average American income is something around seven thousand dollars a year. The average man works for forty years. If he saved only ten cents out of every dollar he earned for himself and his family, he would save twenty-four thousand dollars not counting interest which would more than double it.

Here is an interesting little test you can make. Take the number of years you have been married, times your income, times ten per cent. That is how much you should have in a permanent, never touched, savings program for your later years. If you have this amount or more in your savings account, you belong to the top five per cent of the people in this country. If it is less, you are in the ninety-five per cent boat. This latter is obviously a leaky boat. So by starting a systematic plan now and adding maybe five per cent more of your income, you might be able to catch up pretty fast.

As old Ben Franklin said, "The way to wealth is as plain as the way to market. Waste neither time, nor money, but make the best use of both." Unless you are saving at least ten per cent of your gross income, you may be making a serious mistake.

George Bernard Shaw once said: "I have no use for people who blame circumstances for their position in life. I like people who look for the circumstances they seek, and if they can't find them, make them!"

The way to wealth
depends chiefly
on industry and frugality.

FRANKLIN

Friends, the taxes are indeed very heavy, and if those laid on by the government were the only ones we had to pay, we might more easily discharge them; but we have many others, and much more grievous to some of us. We are taxed twice as much by our idleness, three times as much by our pride, and four times as much by our folly.

FRANKLIN

Work

The Farmer and the Preacher

A favorite story of mine is the one about a preacher who was driving down a country road when he came upon the most magnificent farm he had ever seen in a life spent in rural preaching. The farm stood out like a diamond; it sparkled. While it was by no means a new farm, the house and outbuildings were finely constructed and freshly painted. The garden around the house displayed a collection of beautiful flowers. A fine row of trees lined each side of the white-graveled drive. The fields were beautifully tilled and a fine herd of fat dairy cattle grazed knee-deep in the pasture. All this comprised a beautiful painting of what the ideal farm should look like and the preacher stopped to drink in the sight.

It was then he noticed the farmer on a big, shiny tractor, hard at work. As the farmer approached the spot where the preacher stood beside his car, the preacher hailed him. The farmer stopped his tractor, idled down the engine, and shouted a friendly hello.

And the preacher said to him, "My good man, God has certainly blessed you with a magnificent farm." There was a pause as the farmer took off his billed cap and wiped the perspiration from his face with a bandana. He studied the preacher for a moment and then shifted in his seat to take a look around his pride and joy. Then he turned back to the preacher and said, "Yes, He has, and we're grateful. But you should have seen this place when He had it all to Himself!"

The preacher looked at the strong, friendly features of the farmer for a moment, smiled, and with a wave of his hand, climbed back into his car and continued on his way. He heard the roar of the tractor's engine as the farmer returned to his work and he thought, "That man has given me my sermon for next Sunday."

He thought about the fact that every farmer along this road had been blessed with the same land, the same opportunity, and each worked his farm according to his nature. He understood that every farm, every home of every family in the country was the living reflection of the people who lived there. He understood that the land we are given is not the acres we buy for a farm, or the lot on which we build a home, or the apartment we rent, but rather the life we've been blessed with. That's our plot of ground; that's the land we sow and from which we are then obliged to reap the resulting harvest.

The farmer he had seen would find abundant reward, not just when the time came to gather in his crops, but every time he looked around his place; every time he returned from town to that white-graveled drive and the trees that lined it and the fine home and gardens that waited at the end of it. He was grateful for what he had, but he knew that it is not what is given us that makes the difference, but rather what we do with it, what we make of what we have.

Next to faith in God is faith in labor.

BOVEE

There is a perennial nobleness, even sacredness in work. Were he ever so benighted and forgetful of his high calling, there is always hope in a man who actually and earnestly works.

CARLYLE

The fruit derived from labor is the sweetest of all pleasures.

VAUVENARGUES

Business

A Deeper Purpose

I have long held the belief that every business, no matter what its form or function, should have a purpose beyond that of profit and survival.

Naturally, the first responsibility of management, whether of a small neighborhood restaurant, a corner gas station, or a corporate giant, is to survive and grow. It must earn a profit, not only to satisfy its owner or its stockholders and directors, but also to pump needed money into research, development, and expansion. It must earn a profit so that it can continue to pay the salaries of its employees and offer jobs to more people as the company grows.

But it should also have an additional goal, a deeper purpose constantly before it, and this should be to upgrade all who are influenced by it. I am sure there are many who will smile at this sentiment, but there are also many who will not. The fact is that those who take this idea most seriously are the managers of the world's most successful firms in every field of business.

But in many businesses this second purpose is ignored even if it is recognized or understood. This is precisely why the majority of businesses of all kinds have to be classified as second-rate; they lack the deeper purpose that must accompany greatness in anything. In fact, the not uncommon slump or leveling off, which comes to so many businesses after a long period of growth, is often brought about by the abandonment of this deeper purpose.

For example, a business which begins with a purpose of providing the best product it can offer in its field may, ten or fifteen years later, be more concerned with shaving costs and increasing profit margins. Many once successful business firms have gone under because they became so involved in markets, competition, and pricing that they lost sight of the company's purpose: its reason for being. There is a saying that people remember quality long after they have forgotten price. The most successful companies on earth are those that manage to give top quality at a reasonable price.

Our country proved to the world that it could be done.

Every businessman must ask himself, "How is my customer's life somehow improved, upgraded, bettered because he uses my product or service? What is my contribution to society beyond that of earning a living?"

Similarly a father and mother should ask themselves, "What are we contributing to our children besides food, clothing, school, and shelter?" It is this greater purpose that spells the difference between that which is average and that which is great and none of us can ask that question of ourselves too often.

He that does good to another, does good also to himself, not only in the consequences, but in the very act; for the consequence of well doing is, in itself, ample reward.

SENECA

The old mousetrap story was true a hundred years ago and is true today. If we make the best one, and it is priced right, and we serve a thousand people—we prosper. If we serve a million and do it better than our mousetrap competitors, we prosper a thousand-fold, and not because we are capitalistic. We prosper only because we serve more people better than others; we satisfy their wants; we help them along the way.

HUGHSTON MCBAIN

Self-confidence

A Consciousness of Competence

One night a few years ago I was among a group listening to records. We especially admired a collection of great, traditional songs by a man who has been a star in show business for almost a quarter of a century. Someone said, "That guy's really got it." This triggered a discussion on just what "it" is and why so few have it, while so many do not. What makes a star—not just in show business, but in any field of endeavor?

The man we were listening to was singing the same songs we had all heard hundreds of times.

He was singing the same notes, the same words. Why did he have such a marked effect upon us? What was it about him, as a performer, that made such a difference?

As you think about these questions, apply them to a great golfer who is consistently in the top money, or a great ball player, or salesman, or businessman, or plumber, or doctor, or wife and mother. Ask yourself what is it about these people that makes them a little better than those who are just good.

Well, let me give you my opinion on the matter. To begin, all of these stars are in work which comes close to perfectly matching their natural talents; they are not just round pegs in round holes; rather, they are uniquely shaped pegs which have found perfectly matching, uniquely shaped holes. They take to what they do like a duck takes to water. When they are doing that at which they excel, they are in their element and are happier there than anyplace else. They would be doing what they are doing no matter how much or how little money they made.

To discover whether or not you are in the right line, you need only ask yourself if the same is true of you.

Next, they are wholly dedicated to what they do. Everything else takes second place in their lives. They spend more time, more care, more practice, more thought, more observation upon what they do than do those who are just good, or even very good. I guess you could sum this up by saying they work harder at their specialty than at anything else.

Finally (and it is here that one of the elusive

qualities of real greatness makes its appearance), they know they are good, have supreme confidence in themselves, and, as a result, develop what I call "a consciousness of competence." This is what causes them to relax to the degree necessary for true greatness in anything. While others are nervously straining to excel, forcing themselves and in this forcing falling short, the stars are relaxed in the knowledge of their own greatness. The great painter paints boldly, and the great writer writes the same way; there's no hedging or playing it safe or keeping open an escape route. They burn their bridges behind them in the sure knowledge of victory. They don't always win, but over the years this attitude keeps them in the elite ranks of stardom.

The greatest man is he who chooses right with the most invincible resolution.

SENECA

A really great man is known by three signs—generosity in the design, humanity in the execution, moderation in success.

BISMARCK

If any man seeks for greatness, let him forget greatness and ask for truth, and he will find both.

HORACE MANN

123

Interdependence

You Can't Go It Alone

Have you ever heard someone—usually one very young—say, "I don't need anybody. I'll go it alone"?

I seem to remember saying the same thing myself when I had more ambition than good sense. But the fact is that none of us can go it alone. Even Robinson Crusoe, when he landed on his island, had a good store of knowledge accumulated from books and his contact with others . . . and it saved his life.

As one expert put it, we think and we often say that the new idea or insight is the product of the single human brain. In one sense, it is, but all our creativity today is not a product of an isolated human brain but of a brain conditioned by interaction with other humans and by the history of civilization. What kind of progress could we make in the new thoughts and ideas with which we deal today if mankind had not left us the legacy of language, of numbers, of symbolic thinking in general? In fact, without such primitive tools of civilization as pencil and paper, with which we keep records of our thoughts, how far could we progress individually or collectively?

Dr. Ralph W. Gerard tells of a meeting in Berlin between a great English physiologist and a great German physiologist, both eventual Nobel Prize winners. The German, Warburg, was working on the enzymes in cells which make it possible for them to use oxygen and give off carbon dioxide and so get the energy to support their activity. He almost had "the respiratory enzyme," as it has come to be called, but had not quite been able to pin it down chemically. The Englishman, Hill, mentioned an observation just reported at the Physiological Society in England, that light can break up a combination of hemoglobin and carbon monoxide. This gave the clue. Warburg spent that night in the laboratory, blocking the respiration of yeast in the presence of carbon monoxide and restoring it by strong illumination. The next morning he sent off the paper which brought him a Nobel Prize. His insight and idea were clearly sparked by the communication from another mind. He made an important discovery and deserved his prize, but he probably could not have accomplished it by himself.

The point here is that you just cannot go it alone, and that it is a good idea to develop a sense of the brotherhood of man. As John Donne so beautifully put it: "No man is an island, intire of itselfe; every man is a peece of the Continent, a part of the maine; if a Clod bee washed away by the Sea, Europe is the lesse, as well as if a Promontorie were; as well as if a Mannor of thy friends or of thine owne were; any man's death diminishes me, because I am involved in Mankinde; And therefore never send to know for whom the bell tolls; it tolls for thee."

We need and must depend upon each other to survive and prosper. And since this is true, it should engender in each of us a sense of gratitude to our fellows.

Light is the task when many share the toil.

HOMER

We are members of one great body, planted by nature in a mutual love, and fitted for a social life—we must consider that we were born for the good of the whole.

SENECA

The fact that in Greater New York eight million people have developed ways of working together in peace and dignity is more important than New York's skyscrapers. . . .

DAVID E. LILIENTHAL

Self-improvement

The New Joneses

One of the top people in the field of motivational research—the business of discovering why people do the things they do—is Dr. Ernest Dichter. In an article in the Harvard Business Review, *Dr. Dichter had some interesting things to say.*

For one thing, he said, the once popular phrase "What will the neighbors say?" is becoming obsolete. It appears that we're getting to the point, as persons and as families, where we no longer care what the neighbors say. We've always said *we didn't care, but now it seems we really don't.*

Having enough to eat and a first feel of the gossamer web of security which society is beginning to spin around us, we find that our worries about financial disaster and destitute abandonment have diminished. Instead, we are beginning to discover a new form of discontent, for it is human nature that when we have sighted one goal on the horizon, we begin to wonder what might lie beyond and to strive for the further promise.

For thousands of years we worked for food and shelter. During this period, prestige in the form of wealth was a sort of psychological armor intended to discourage the enemy from attacking us. It proved we were powerful adversaries.

For instance, the fur of the beast or the scalp of the enemy slain used to be the trophy of the hunter. It stated clearly to all competitors, "I am mighty and strong. Don't challenge me." Today fur in the form of a mink coat bought for the female and paraded on her shoulders is still a symbol of prowess. It speaks an eloquent language understood by the Joneses up and down the street. Keeping up with the Joneses has been a way of warning the Joneses not to make the mistake of pegging us too low. We surround ourselves with symbols of power bought with the measure of our personal might—the dollar.

Lately, though, this simple game seems to have been disturbed by a new Jones who clamors to be kept up with. Now we're hearing from the "Inner Jones." For example, a recent study turned up the fact that people are much less concerned with the possession of furniture which will impress their neighbors than with pieces which will please them personally. Furniture is now being bought to be lived with and on, rather than simply to be shown off. And this holds true for every other possession.

The most striking phenomenon of our consumer rebellion is the search for inner satisfaction. Studies show that people are groping for real values and discovering them, not in material possessions, but in self-development—the realization of self-potential. Moving forward, improving oneself, and being better today than yesterday are beginning to be the real goals of life.

From here on out, it will not be so much a matter of what we have in the way of possessions—we'll all have those. Instead, the person who more truly becomes himself, who does the best job of developing his innate potential, will be the one admired by the "new Joneses."

What do you suppose will satisfy the soul except to walk free and own no superior?

LAWS FOR CREATIONS

Those who are quite satisfied sit still and do nothing; those who are not quite satisfied are the sole benefactors of the world.

LANDOR

There have been a few moments when
I have known complete satisfaction,
but only a few. I have rarely been
free from the disturbing realization
that my playing might have been better.

JAN IGNACE PADEREWSKI

Persistence

Failure Can Be Good

Has life ever shown you that the right to fail is as important as the right to succeed? If we didn't have bad weather, we would never appreciate sunny days. One hardly ever values his good health until he becomes ill. And I have never known a successful man or woman whose success did not hinge on some failure or another.

There is an old saying which goes, "It is impossible to succeed without suffering. If you are successful and have not suffered, someone has suffered for you; and if you are suffering, without succeeding, it is so that someone may succeed after you. But there is no success without suffering."

Success in the world, any kind of success, is like a universal college degree. It can only be earned by following a certain course of action for a definite period of time. It is impossible for real success to be easy. Success also follows a kind of natural selection. Only those individuals who are willing to try again after their failures, those who refuse to let defeat keep them down for long, those who seem to have some strange inner knowledge that success can be theirs if they just stay with it long enough, finally win their diploma in life.

Most men and women who have earned success will tell you that often, just as they felt they were finally reaching the point in life on which they had set their hearts, the rug was pulled out from under them and they found themselves back at the starting line again, and not just once or twice, but many times.

Thus only those of patient persistence are rewarded. But those who do not achieve great success in life are by no means failures. They are successful in their way because they have what they really want. They simply did not want great success enough. They're happy with what they've got—and there is nothing wrong with that.

One day a young man came to my office and told me he wanted very much to make a great success of himself. He asked if I could show him the secret.

I told him to decide definitely upon what he considered success to be for him, and then work at it for twelve to sixteen hours a day until he had achieved it. And when he wasn't working at it, to think about it. By doing this, he could reach his goal in perhaps five years or so. However, to achieve success, he must force himself back on the track every time he strayed off, realizing that failures are as necessary to success as an excavation is to a basement.

I never saw that young man again. I wonder if he took my advice. It is an unusual person whose desire is larger than his distaste for the work involved.

Successful people are dreamers who have found a dream too exciting, too important, to remain in the realm of fantasy. Day by day, hour by hour, they toil in the service of their dream until they can see it with their eyes and touch it with their hands.

A man learns little from victory; much from defeat.

CHINESE PROVERB

Success does not consist in never making mistakes but in never making the same one a second time.

G. B. SHAW

We often discover what will succeed by finding out what will not.
Probably he who never made a mistake never made a discovery.

ANONYMOUS

Business

Big Business Started Small

These days we hear a lot about big business and how much bigger it is getting. But there is nothing wrong with expansion, and one of the most interesting things about it is that every business, no matter how big it might be today, started small. One of the largest corporations in the United States was started with only a few thousand dollars of borrowed money, and after ten years of operation had only six thousand dollars to its credit. And another good thing to remember is that every business, no matter how big or far-flung, no matter how many thousands of employees or how many skyscraper office buildings it may have, got its start in the mind of one human being.

Committees have their place when it comes to considering and solving problems. But every good idea had to start in the mind of one human being and usually came as the result of something he observed. You could start a business of your own this year which in twenty or thirty years could be a growing, far-flung industrial empire, too. People who tell you all the good businesses are taken, or that there are no more opportunities, are wrong.

Six words lie at the root of any business success: FIND A NEED AND FILL IT! The extent of your success will be determined by the need's importance and your ability to fill that need.

Whenever you see a business that is thriving and successful, you may be sure it is filling a need. If it were not, it would just stop and close up shop. The size of a business is controlled only by the number of people it serves and the extent of the need it fills.

I know a man who found his success running a gas station. One day he was watching a customer and noticed that while the man's car was being serviced he had nothing to do but stand around and wait. He had money to spend and there were undoubtedly things he would like to buy, things he needed if he could only see them. So my friend started adding these things. He kept right on adding them until now he has built a big sporting-goods store alongside his now large and modern gas station. While your car is being serviced at his station, you can buy anything from a package of gum to a two-hundred-dollar shotgun, or a boat and trailer, or a box of chocolates for your wife. You can also cash a check any time you feel like it, and he extends credit on everything. On a Friday or Saturday he will cash forty to fifty thousand dollars in checks each day; and hardly anyone leaves without buying something.

My friend's business was no different from any other gas station in the country until he saw a need and filled it. He could sell out today for half a million dollars. The fact is that there is more opportunity today, far more, than there ever was before. We just have to be able to see it.

A wise man will make more opportunities than he finds.

BACON

It is common to overlook what is near by keeping the eye fixed on something remote. In the same manner present opportunities are neglected and attainable good is slighted by minds busied in extensive ranges and intent upon future advantages.

SAMUEL JOHNSON

The talent of success is nothing more than doing what you can do well, and doing well whatever you do . . .

LONGFELLOW

136

Marriage

How's Your Conversation?

The experts claim that one of the most serious problems of marriage and one of the prime causes for its failure is the inability or reluctance on the part of husbands and wives to talk to each other.

It seems the longer two people live together, the more they tend to take one another for granted. It's like driving a brand-new car—at first it's exciting and interesting, but with time, well, it's just a car. People are not machines, and this kind of attitude toward a wife or a husband is deadly to a happy marriage. A couple with such an attitude might put on the appearance of marriage, but it is only a matter of a contract and convenience.

If there is anyone on earth to whom you can talk, and with enjoyment, it should be the person you have married. The problem seems to come from "letting down." Home becomes a kind of cave where a person feels he doesn't have to behave himself; he can just let go completely. This may be all right for the person living alone, but it never works when two people are living together.

For an intelligent, considerate person, the home should be as important as the office. If a man does his best all day to be courteous and cheerful in order to get along with the people with whom he works, why should he feel that he doesn't have to make the same effort at home? A wife is so much more important than the boys at the office, or the girls, that one would think he'd go out of his way to be charming, interesting, cheerful, and, in general, quite a guy.

The same is true for the wife. If she is having some of the girls over for a luncheon, she is really on the ball. She selects the food with care, cooks it the same way, sets the table with her best china and silver, sees that her hair looks nice and that she is well dressed. All during lunch she is gay, witty, perfectly charming; she is a sympathetic listener and she laughs at anything with even a remote hint of humor.

But what happens when Clyde comes home? Does she give the breadwinner the same treatment? Does she make it a point to look her best? She does, if she is smart. He too should rate the best silver. He is the most important person in her life, isn't he?

Now we come back to this business of conversation, the point on which the experts say so many marriages break down. What does she have to say? Well, what she should talk about, at least at first, are all the nice things that happened during the day; the funny thing that little Clyde, Jr., did, or how pleasant it is to have a fine husband. Anything, so long as it's cheerful. She should not unload her problems the minute her husband comes home. She can talk about the news, a magazine story she read; ask him what happened during the day.

Surprisingly, even people who understand the importance of good conversation sometimes fail to recognize its place in the home. A man and his wife should have more to talk about than any two people on earth. And all it takes is a little effort, and an awareness of just how important it is.

She was a phantom of delight
When first she gleamed upon my sight;

A perfect woman, nobly planned,
To warn, to comfort, and command.

William Wordsworth

A man of sense and education should meet
a suitable companion in a wife. It is

a miserable thing when the conversation can only be such as to whether the mutton should be boiled or roasted, and probably a dispute about that.

SAMUEL JOHNSON

140

Service

The Man on the White Horse

During the depression, when millions of Americans were daily forming long lines outside employment offices and signs reading NO HELP WANTED *appeared in thousands of business windows, do you know what words were most often heard by businessmen? Practically all the people looking for work said the same thing: "Give me a job; I'll do anything." That is why they had so much trouble finding work.*

In the first place, the depression had put a crimp in most businesses. Thousands folded, and those which remained through good management and necessary products and services were mostly cutting back on the number of their employees rather than looking for more. The one thing in the world they were not looking for was someone who said, "Give me a job; I'll do anything."

But a man I know solved the problem for himself. He found out how to get a job during the toughest part of the depression, in just about any business he chose, by a surprisingly simple and logical method.

When he found himself one of the millions out of a job and with a family to support, he began to think about it. He asked himself, "What does the businessman need today more than anything else?" The only logical answer to that was more business.

So my friend chose the line of business in which he was most interested and where he felt he could help the most. He then began studying that business. He spent weeks learning all he could about it, pursuing his research in the public library. He would even go to a man in that business and spend hours talking with him about the business problems brought on by the depression and the shortage of money. He spent this whole time racking his brain for ideas which could be of help, seeking ways and means of improving and increasing trade. One of the most amazing things he learned was that his weeks of study, talking, and research resulted in his knowing as much, and in some cases more, about the business as the men he talked to. [They were mostly waiting for something good to develop, while he was actively engaged in doing something about it himself.]

When he felt he was ready and had gathered together some really original ideas, he went to the president of one of the major companies and said, "I believe I know several ways your business can be increased and your profit picture improved. I'd like to work with you on it."

Here was a man who, instead of asking for a job and saying he would do anything, appeared as a "man on a white horse" offering to help a business keep alive and actually increase its profits. Needless to say, he got the job and sailed through the depression without any more trouble. You would be surprised at the number of businesses looking for such a man on a white horse, even today; but you would be equally surprised how few candidates there are.

People are always talking about originality; but what do they mean? As soon as we are born, the world begins to work upon us and this goes on to the end. After all, what can we call our own, except energy, strength, and will.

GOETHE

Originality is simply a pair of fresh eyes.

T. W. HIGGINSON

Ignorance

What You Don't Know *Will* Hurt You

"What you don't know won't hurt you." I often wonder where this old saying began.

I can imagine cases where it might be true, but I can also think of a lot more where it would be false. By and large, what you don't know *will* hurt you. In fact, at least as it applies to our so-called civilized society, it can be said that a person will be hurt or at least seriously handicapped by the extent of his ignorance. Each year thousands of people are killed, hundreds of thousands are injured, millions are hurt, embarrassed, or find their marriages going to pot because they lack wisdom, insight, or even information.

Just as a child can be terribly burned because in his simple ignorance he pulls a boiling pot off the stove, an adult lives in jeopardy due to his ignorance of the laws of nature, the law of averages, or the laws of men and things.

Take the person who habitually drives at high speed—for whom speed limit signs are for others as are signs for school zones and residential areas. In his ignorance, which he believes is ability or confidence, he must and will eventually suffer. He is pushing the law of averages a little further every time he gets into his car. It has to catch up with him sooner or later.

In marriage the person who takes delight in poking fun at his mate in the presence of others will eventually come to a reckoning, as will the perennial criticizer . . . or complainer . . . or shouter. Like drops of water on stone, our transgressions wear away the seemingly indestructible surface until finally it cracks. What we don't know *will* hurt us. I overheard two women talking in a restaurant the other day. One of them, an extremely attractive woman of about forty, who unfortunately talked a trifle too loudly, said, "I fell in love with him even though I recognized his faults. But eventually those faults caused me to fall out of love and I divorced him."

The greatest love can be destroyed, as was the Alexandrian Library, by ignorance. The fact that something is great and beautiful in no way protects it from stupidity. Nothing really happens by accident. Everything, without exception, is the result of cause and effect. If we are intelligent and have made it our business to know as much as we can about this business of living successfully, at least as successfully as possible in the short time we are given, we will see to it that our causes are right—knowing that the effects will take care of themselves.

If we drive our cars with respect for the laws of man and nature, we enormously increase our chances of survival. By keeping our cars under constant control we can avoid being killed by those who drive with ignorant abandon.

And if we will say and do things toward those we love which tend to deepen and increase that love, rather than destroy it, we can continue to earn and keep their love. As Huxley said, "We will be punished for our ignorance just as quickly as for willful disobedience." So, in my book, what you don't know *will* hurt you. People are being destroyed every day in hundreds of ways that prove the point.

Better be unborn than untaught,
for ignorance is the root of misfortune.

PLATO

In the natural world ignorance is visited
as willful disobedience, incapacity meets the
same punishment as crime.—Nature's punishment
is not even a word and a blow and the blow first,

but the blow without the word.—It is left for the sufferer to find out why the blow was given.

THOMAS H. HUXLEY

It is not the crook we fear but the honest man who doesn't know what he is doing.

OWEN D. YOUNG

Worry

Seven Blocks of Fog

As two young recruits in basic training were talking about expected orders, one confessed that he was worried sick about the possibility of being shipped overseas. The other recruit, an amateur philosopher, said to him, "There's no sense worrying about it." His friend asked, "How do you figure that?"

"It's this way," said the philosopher. "There's a fifty-fifty chance you won't go overseas. If you don't, you've nothing to worry about. If you do, there's a fifty-fifty

chance you won't see action. If you don't you've nothing to worry about. If you do, there's a fifty-fifty chance you won't get shot. If you don't, there's nothing to worry about. If you do, there's a fifty-fifty chance you won't be killed. If not, no worries. If you are *killed, you won't have any more worries. So why worry in the first place?"*

I don't know if this appeased the worried soldier, but it represents a sound attitude. And if you will reduce the things you worry about to the size they deserve, your worries may well approach the vanishing point.

I remember reading that a dense fog, blanketing seven city blocks to a depth of one hundred feet, could be put in a single water glass. That is, all the moisture, the water droplets, in a dense fog covering seven city blocks to a depth of one hundred feet, could be held in a single water tumbler.

Worry is a lot like that. Worry is a fog that can cloud our vision, knock our perspective out of kilter, and slow us down to a shuffling, halting, walk. But like fog, if most of our worries were reduced to their real size, they could all be placed in a water glass.

Experts have estimated that of all the things we worry about, forty per cent will never happen; thirty per cent are past and all the worry in the world cannot change them; twelve per cent are needless worries about our health; ten per cent are petty, miscellaneous worries, leaving eight per cent for things that legitimately deserve our concern and thought.

This means that ninety-two per cent of the things you worry about, if you tend to be something of a worrier, will never happen. They are either in the past or do not deserve your attention.

The trick is to winnow the eight per cent from the one hundred per cent. And I suppose this is where being well adjusted, or at least better adjusted, helps. It might be of some comfort to learn that as we get older one of the really great compensations is that we tend to worry less. Gradually, through the years, we learn for ourselves what the experts try to tell us: that just about all of our concerns solve themselves one way or another or disappear before they get to us.

Looking at our worries *en masse* makes them seem impenetrable. It's like looking at a large crowd of people we must pass through. When we enter the crowd, however, we find we need only pass by one person at a time and that soon we are out on the other side.

Telling someone not to worry is ridiculous. But if you tell him the story of the fog, or that only eight per cent of his worries really deserve his thought and attention, you can usually help him toward a more realistic perspective.

Worry is interest paid on trouble before it comes due.

W. R. INGE

I have never met a healthy person who

worried very much about his health, or a really good person who worried much about his own soul.

J. B. S. HALDANE

Worry affects the circulation—the heart, the glands, the whole nervous system. I have never known a man who died from overwork, but many who died from doubt.

DR. CHARLES MAYO

Enthusiasm

Lose It, and You're Finished!

About the worst thing that can happen to a human being is to lose his enthusiasm, his excitement, his zest for living.

It has long been a belief of mine that the person who maintains an air of somber boredom, that know-it-all, there's-nothing-new-under-the-sun attitude, is a person with deep and serious feelings of personal inadequacy.

Enthusiasm can be so easily lost. In trying

to imitate their elders, which is a serious mistake made by virtually all children (it should be the other way around most of the time), young people often adopt a pose and an expression which seems to say, "Nothing can surprise, charm, or interest me in the slightest." Hands in pockets, leaning against a wall, head tilted slightly back, and viewing an uninteresting world through half-closed eyes, the teen-ager believes he is the image of the experienced, sophisticated man-of-the-world whose most pressing problem is stifling a yawn.

It would not come as a complete surprise to me if most of this is caused by the tendency of the average adult to try to give the impression to his children that he knows everything in the world worth knowing. How many times has a youngster run with eager, excited face to his father or mother with some new fact, only to have it waved off with a comment such as, "Yes, yes, I know all about that," or "Are you just discovering that?"

Ego-pricking of this kind can go a long way toward emptying a child's tank of enthusiasm. So, maybe he makes the mistake of trying to grow up to be like his mother or father. Maybe he is too young to realize that if they are living dull, uninteresting lives, it is because they have permitted themselves to become dull, uninteresting people.

But the person who keeps his enthusiasm goes through life with his wonder, excitement, and interest at a consistently high level. As a parent, he is quick to admit to his children that he does not know very much about anything yet and neither does anybody else. He understands the vital importance of fostering and feeding the enthusiasm of youth; he teaches his youngsters that so-called "know-it-alls" are to be pitied, or laughed at, but seldom listened to.

The pity of it is that our enthusiasm never dies a natural death. We murder enthusiasm through slow strangulation by imitating the dull, uninteresting people who already have strangled their own natural enthusiasm.

It is a sad day when the curiosity, excitement, and zest for living go out of one's life. There is so much in the world to see and know about, there is so much to do, so much to give, that the loss of enthusiasm for living can only come from a kind of mental blindness. I, for one, hope to keep my enthusiasm—and myself—alive.

Whenever you see a person affecting an attitude of bored sophistication, you can rest assured that the attitude is phony and the person has a lot of growing younger to do.

Every production of genius must be the production of enthusiasm.

DISRAELI

Every great and commanding movement in the annals of the world is the triumph of enthusiasm. Nothing great was ever achieved without it.

EMERSON

You can do nothing effectually without enthusiasm.

GUIZOT

154

Giving

The Secret of Happiness

Every now and then something is said that affects you like an itch in a place where you cannot scratch. One such remark that I would like to pass along to you here, I heard in California while attending the funeral of someone who was very close to me.

As I stood on the rolling California foothills in the shade of a row of tall eucalyptus trees, I heard these words: "Fear not that your life shall come to an end but rather that it shall never have a beginning."

The woman, whose death had brought me to California, had had a beginning in life. She had also accomplished a great deal and was loved by all who knew her. In fact, it was recalling her life that made me think of others whose lives contrasted so sharply, of people who lived solely for themselves. Since their "what's-in-it-for-me" attitude had never sown a single seed, they reaped a barren harvest all their lives.

These are the world's most unfortunate people. That they don't give of themselves to others hurts very few, but the unhappiness they bring to themselves is great. We will all know sorrow from time to time, as I did that day in California. But sorrow is one thing; unhappiness is something else.

Running the risk of oversimplifying, I think it can be said that a person is unhappy to the extent that he fails to give of himself to others.

This puts happiness, well-being, and peace of mind within the reach of everyone. They can be found in the simplest dwelling or the greatest mansion. They will be found wherever there is a person who has discovered for himself either through long contemplation, or the good fortune of being raised in a happy family, that to get, we must give.

If we give with no thought of getting, there is no limit to the abundance that will accrue to us. We limit our happiness to the extent that we try to measure out happiness to others.

Few of us, of course, are real experts in this. It is the most natural thing in the world, it seems, to ask ourselves, "Now just what am I going to get out of this?" It is hard for us to realize that it is not what we get but rather what we enjoy that makes life interesting and fulfilling.

The little lady whose body was in the flower-draped casket that afternoon in California had known this all her life. Her life had been filled with laughter and good cheer all the sixty-nine years, three months, and twenty-two days of her lifetime. What a wonderful way to live! And what a wonderful legacy to leave to those who knew her and who knew the secret of her happiness.

Whenever we think only of ourselves, it's like drawing blinds to shut out the sunlight.

Or what man is there of you, whom if his son ask bread, will he give him a stone.

MATTHEW 7:9

(*You give but little when you give of your possessions. It is when you give of yourself that you truly give.*)

GIBRAN

Give what you have. To some it may be better than you dare think.

LONGFELLOW

Purpose

How Deep Do You Go?

Occasionally a strange sight is seen at sea. The wind, the tide, and the surface ice will all be going in one direction, but moving majestically against these forces will be an iceberg. The reason is not hard to find. We see only a small part of the iceberg. Deep down in the water is the base, controlled by more powerful, deeper currents.

Strength of character is the powerful current that keeps us going in the right direction.

People are like icebergs, large and small. The little ones which float on the surface are subject to any wind or superficial current that happens along. They go first this way and then that along with all the other things which float on the surface. Their roots do not go deep enough to be gripped by the currents that will give their lives direction and purpose. These people lack a meaningful philosophy of life.

I think everyone, from time to time, should ask himself, "Where am I going? Am I living in such a way to bring lasting, important benefits to myself and those who depend upon me? Am I honestly proud of the job I'm doing and the manner in which I have been conducting myself?"

More people should realize that each of us needs a settled purpose in life, an aiming point. Then by doing our very best every day, we will reach this point on which we have set our compass. In this way, we can sail along on course regardless of the winds which may come up. And we need take no notice of the flurries of unrest, indecision, and short-term expediency we see about us. It is the long-term profit which is the lasting profit. By going first this way and then that, we will ultimately arrive nowhere. We will find ourselves, eventually, right back where we started, while the big people, with their bases in the deep currents, have long since disappeared over the horizon on the way to their goals.

As Carlyle put it: "A man with a half-volition goes backwards and forwards and makes no way on the smoothest road; a man with a whole volition advances on the roughest and will reach his purpose, if there be even a little wisdom in it." He also said: "The man without a purpose is like a ship without a rudder; a waif; a nothing; a no man. Have a purpose in life, and, having it, throw such strength of mind and muscle into your work as God has given you."

A good way to start is to try to become as good as you can at what you are now doing. No matter what your job happens to be, it will take on additional dignity and meaning if you do it as well as you possibly can. Any other attitude can only result in your developing a poor opinion of yourself, in dissatisfaction and frustration. Becoming outstanding at what you do is a purpose worthy of any man or woman and will result in your developing the deep roots you seek.

T. T. Munger wrote: "There is no road to success but through a clear, strong purpose. Nothing can take its place. A purpose underlies character, culture, position, attainment of every sort."

It is in men as in soils where sometimes there is a vein of gold which the owner knows not of.

SWIFT

We are not that we are, nor do we treat or esteem each other for such, but for that we are capable of being.

THOREAU

Friendship

Do Them a Favor

A good friend of mine came up with an interesting comment the other day. He had recently taken a business problem to a friend in a different business and had asked for help in working it out. He then told his friend that he was doing him a favor by pushing his problem upon him and that he would be happy to have the favor returned by helping with any business problems his friend might have in the future.

I had never thought about doing someone a favor by giving him one of my problems, but the more you think about it, the truer this becomes. There are several good reasons.

1. If he is really a friend, he is glad to help you with your problems. He welcomes the opportunity.

2. By giving him your problem, you are forcing him to think, which is the highest function of a human being.

3. You are making him think along lines with which he is probably not familiar, which stretches his mind and develops his creativity.

4. You make him realize you consider his opinions of value, and this cannot help but make him feel important.

5. By helping you with a solution to your problem, he just might come up with some excellent ideas regarding his own life and business.

I remember reading about Benjamin Franklin having a rather powerful enemy in Philadelphia. For some reason, this person didn't like Dr. Franklin and made no bones about it. In trying to come up with a way of turning this enemy into a friend, Dr. Franklin hit on the idea of asking him to lend a particular book he knew him to have. He found that the man was happy to do so, and with this break in the cold war which had existed between them, they soon became the best of friends.

Asking for help is the best way to make the person who is asked feel important, needed, and respected. It is a fact that you are actually doing him a favor.

A man named Hall once wrote: "A friend should be one in whose understanding and virtue we can equally confide, and whose opinion we can value at once for its justness and its sincerity.

He who has made the acquisition of a judicious and sympathizing friend may be said to have doubled his mental resources."

William Penn wrote: "A true friend unbosoms freely, advises justly, assists readily, adventures boldly, takes all patiently, defends courageously, and continues a friend unchangeably."

You can say that a true and loyal friendship is an exceedingly rare and wonderful thing—like a happy marriage or a successful partnership. It needs attention, care, guarding, and above all, it needs to be needed.

True friendship is a plant of slow growth and must undergo and withstand the shocks of adversity before it is entitled to the appellation.

WASHINGTON

The firmest friendships have been formed in mutual adversity; as iron is most strongly united by the fiercest flame.

COLTON

Life is to be fortified by many friendships. To love and be loved is the greatest happiness of existence.

SYDNEY SMITH

Opportunity

Obey That Impulse

Refusing to obey our impulses often keeps us from having a lot of fun and perhaps from doing a lot of things we should be doing.

Have you noticed that from time to time, for no particularly good reason, you will get a sudden impulse—feel a sudden urge? Everything about the idea seems good at the moment; you can't find a thing wrong with it. But instead of acting on the impulse right then, you wait, you sit back and begin thinking about it critically. Pretty soon you can find a lot of reasons for not doing it, or it just passes, and an opportunity is gone forever.

These sudden impulses often come straight out of our subconscious minds, giving us valuable direction—direction we should be taking. By vetoing them, we miss all kinds of opportunities. Dr. William Moulton Marston, a consulting psychologist, says that most people stifle enough good impulses during the course of a day to change the current of their lives. These inner flashes light up their minds for an instant and set them all aglow with the stimulation of the thing. But then they lapse back into the old routine, apparently content to bask in the afterglow which the impulse has provided and content to feel that maybe later on they might do something about it. On this very subject William James said, "Every time a resolve or fine glow of feeling evaporates without bearing fruit, it is worse than a chance lost; it works to hinder future emotions from taking the normal path of discharge."

At one point in his career Dr. Marston was employed by a Hollywood motion picture studio where he worked with Walter B. Pitkin. One day they were presented with an ambitious production idea from a young promoter. The plan appealed to both of them, but they reacted differently. While Marston was mulling the thing over, Pitkin picked up a telephone and started dictating a lengthy telegram to a friend in Wall Street. The telegram was almost a yard long when it was delivered, but it carried conviction. As a result of Pitkin's spur-of-the-moment impulse, a ten-million-dollar underwriting of a new motion picture was brought about.

Calvin Coolidge remains an enigma to political commentators because the reasons for his actions were seldom apparent and the source of his shrewdness could not be traced. Almost none of our presidents would seem to have been less impulsive than Calvin Coolidge, but the truth is that he literally trained himself to rely on hunches. As a young attorney in a country law firm, he was interviewing a client one day when he received a telephone call and learned that a county political boss was in town. Without hesitation, he cut short his interview and decided to see this man about proposing himself as a candidate for the legislature. The impulse bore fruit and from then on the inner urges of Calvin Coolidge led him consistently from one political success to another.

A sudden impulse to do something you know you ought not to do should be stifled. But when one of those great hunches pops into your mind, act on it right away or you may miss your opportunity forever.

There is a tide in the affairs of men, which,
taken at the flood, leads on to fortune.

SHAKESPEARE

To improve the golden moment of opportunity,
and catch the good that is within our reach,
is the great art of life.

SAMUEL JOHNSON

All our progress is an unfolding like the vegetable bud. You have first an instinct, then an opinion, then a knowledge, as the plant has root, bud and fruit. Trust the instinct to the end, though you can render no reason.

EMERSON

Memory

Memory Is Good—and Bad

Everything in nature has two sides: a good and a bad, a positive and a negative. In philosophy this thought goes back thousands of years to the Chinese Yin and Yang. The Yang is the good, the sunny side of the hill; the Yin is the dark. There is a dualism in everything in the universe. The rain that waters and fertilizes the crops also brings floods; the fire that warms our homes and cooks our meals causes widespread havoc when out of control. We are familiar with the dualism of love and hate.

Have you ever thought about the good and the bad sides of memory? Each of us really has a very short memory. Yes, the subconscious remembers everything, but the conscious mind forgets. We forget our failures, our mistakes, our foolishness, the pain we have caused, the opportunities we have missed, the love we have failed to give when it was needed. These things pass from our conscious memories as from filters to which they have clung for a while before being washed away by time.

We also forget, unfortunately, the good, and that is bad. We forget the principles, the systems which, if we would but live by them, would result in our achieving the things we seek. We literally forget how to live successfully.

If, through some diabolical device, we were constantly reminded of all our past weaknesses and mistakes, we would live in a state of constant depression, fear, and sorrow—a hell on earth. Instead, our conveniently forgetful minds save us from this.

If, through some wonderful agency, we could be constantly reminded only of the good, of those principles and systems which we know work to our benefit and the benefit of society, we would live in a state of optimism, enthusiasm, and hope. We would go from one success to another.

It is true that the world's most successful people manage to live in this latter state. They are always aware of what they are doing and where they are going. They know that if they will just do certain things a certain way, every day, they will be led to their chosen goals.

Most news seems to be bad. Our newspapers and newscasts are not—and cannot be—filled with all the good that is going on in the world. They report all the *news,* and the great majority of it seems to be on the negative side: the war, murders, crime, disasters, accidents, swindles, scandals. Furthermore, so many of the people around us, subtly influencing us, are so constituted, or so lacking in the proper education, that they too seem to act and talk on the negative side most of the time. If we live then in accordance with our environment, we too will tend more and more to forget the good and dwell on the bad. This means we will live the major part of our lives on the dark side of the ancient Chinese hill.

What is the solution? It is to find a way to remind ourselves every day, as do the really successful, of those things that lead to success, to good. Otherwise, we will forget the good, along with the bad.

A good airplane pilot carefully follows a checklist before taking off and landing; he does this regardless of his hours in the air. It keeps him successful and alive. You and I need a checklist too, every morning and every night.

*Memory is a capricious and arbitrary creature.
You can never tell what pebbles she will pick
up from the shore of life to keep among
her treasures . . .*

HENRY VAN DYKE

*We have committed the Golden Rule to
memory. Let us now commit it to life.*

EDWIN MARKHAM

Morale

It Filters Down From the Top

Have you ever heard the expression "to raise morale"? It's an expression frequently heard in the military service and in organizations of all kinds. But when you stop to think about it a minute, you realize it's a misstatement: morale is not raised from the bottom; it filters down from the top.

The employees of a business, and it makes little difference whether it's the corner supermarket or the largest corporation, will always faithfully reflect the attitude of the person in charge.

In the Navy you'll hear the expression "It's a happy ship." A happy ship is invariably one with a happy skipper. And, strange as it may at first seem, the happiest ship is usually the one that is also the most efficient and performs best. Good morale is not caused by loose, easy discipline. Frequently, just the reverse is true.

A happy skipper is the kind of person who not only realizes the importance of discipline, but also the importance of fairness in all things. He is tough when he needs to be tough, but most of all, he is competent—knows his business and likes his job. Everybody on the ship admires him for both qualities and will try to emulate him. His crew will knock themselves out to please him and fight hard for him in a tight spot.

In a business firm, people in the lower echelons will never complain of discipline if they know it is fair and if they have a hard-working leader who teaches by his own example.

A relaxing of rules and discipline almost always works in a way opposite to what you might expect; it causes morale to drop. Children also need and want discipline of the kind they know to be fair and logical. Without it, they suffer a loss in personal esteem. Letting a child do exactly as he pleases, when he has neither the maturity nor wisdom for such responsibility, is unfair and harmful. It results in a kind of juvenile anarchy and a great deal of unhappiness and frustration for the child. I am not comparing employees with children, but the same principle holds true with employees from the president and vice-presidents all the way down to the boy in the mail room. The president is a kind of company father whose attitude will be reflected throughout the entire organization.

This is interesting to know because you can tell what kind of person is at the head of a company by observing the attitudes of the employees. When you see people loafing on the job, it is not a sign of good but rather of poor morale. It shows weak and ineffective leadership. If you want to know how good a leader is, don't watch him—watch the people under him. People have a tendency to do no more than is required. The paradox is that the less that is required of them, the unhappier they become.

A person's feeling of worth is closely linked to the way in which he is required to handle his job. The type of person who is a natural leader is the one who requires the best of himself.

> *When you know men and you know how to handle men, you've licked the problem of running a business. The executive's job is to provide the kind of leadership that develops the best efforts of the men under him.*
>
> ROY W. MOORE

> *The employer generally gets the employees he deserves.*
>
> SIR WALTER GILBEY

Self-improvement

The End-of-the-Roaders

In the world of business today there is a man we might call the end-of-the-roader. Surprisingly enough, he is often found in the professions as well as in every part of the business community. This is the man who believes, often unconsciously, that he knows enough and no longer needs to learn or to change.

He takes for granted that his company, his profession, his community, and his nation should continue to move ahead and grow and expand with the changing world. He would be horrified if his company, or the companies in which he has perhaps invested his money, shut down their research and development departments. He knows that their future growth and prosperity depend upon never-ending research and the development of new and better ways of doing business.

But what about him? Well, he is personally exempt from all this. He feels that he has accomplished more than his peers and has become a finished product. Well, he is finished all right, but not the way he thinks. The man in business today who does not have a continuing program of study and self-improvement is obsolete, whether he recognizes the fact or not.

And so is the wife who adopts this end-of-the-road attitude. Perhaps it used to be true that all a woman needed was a pretty face and a good figure. Then, if she had sense enough to keep her mouth shut for the next fifty years or so, she could squeak through, maybe. But such is no longer the case.

Young women, the girls in school today, need to realize (and I am sure a good percentage of them do) that the changes in the world that have made a man's job so much more demanding also affect women. An intelligent wife is as important to a man of ambition as an intelligent husband is to a woman. Why should marriage be a one-way street?

Wives will often complain that they do not have time to keep up with the rapidly changing world. Taking care of the house, chauffeuring the kids around, playing bridge with the girls, shopping and planning meals, and all the rest of the activities their schedules include don't allow them the time or energy to improve their minds. But this is a pretty flimsy alibi; one only need consult the national statistics on television viewing to refute this. Any person can find *some* time every day for self-improvement. And every person knows, or certainly should know, the areas in which he or she can stand some improvement.

Many women, it turns out, feel that once they are out of school there is no need for further study and learning; so they stop right there. And I mean they stop. In two or three years they are two or three years behind the times. They confine their reading to light fiction and the women's pages of magazines and newspapers, and gradually, since they are not learning anything new, they begin to forget even the little they learned in school. They become vapid, dull, uninteresting, unexciting. And if their husbands are going to get anywhere in the world, they have to drag their wives along behind them like sea anchors.

For a woman youthful beauty lasts, at best, for only a few years. It is the last thing she should count upon for an interesting, exciting, and rewarding life. And the man should look upon the woman he wants to marry in exactly this light.

The things taught in schools and colleges are not an education, but the means of education.

EMERSON

Anyone who stops learning is old, whether this

happens at twenty or eighty. Anyone who keeps on learning not only remains young but also becomes constantly more valuable.

HARVEY ULLMAN

Self-determination

Life Is Like the Movies

The late Mike Todd once said: "Life is like the movies. We produce our own show." I had never looked at it exactly in that light before, but the thought makes for interesting speculation. It's true; just as there are any number of kinds and types of motion pictures written and produced, you can probably think of people you know or have heard about who have lived every possible story line.

There are the gloomy, gray, and foreboding tragedies that reach into the lives of others and stain everything with a sable or sanguine hue. It's painful to say that the actors in these tragedies have produced their own show, but that seems to be the way it is.

Conversely, and happily, there are the cheerful, warm, and friendly homes, filled with busy, lighthearted people, and they form bright oases in their neighborhoods. There are the low comedies, the strong purposeful, sober stories, the B pictures, and the C pictures, too. These latter feature dull characters who make you sorry you came every time you are in their company. I once overheard a woman make the comment that when her daughter left home to go to college, she and her husband had to learn how to talk to each other. All those years wasted in grinding dullness and lack of love.

Unfortunately, there are the psychopathic stories as well, and the horror stories, and the murder mysteries. There are westerns and detective stories. There is Hamlet played all over again in a thousand families every year; and Romeo and Juliet, and all the other old ubiquitous themes.

So Mike Todd was right: Life *is* like the movies, for the movies are taken from life. What kind of picture does your family project to the world? Is it the kind you would pay to see, or would you pass it up to see one with more interest, excitement, and adventure? Is it warm and friendly and filled with love? Or is it dull and flat and uninteresting? Remember, you are the producer. And as a producer once said to me: "There are no small parts, just small actors."

Any part can be made better, good, or even great, through the talent and effort of the actor. If you find the motion picture you are living uninteresting, don't blame your wife or husband, or the neighbors, or your work. Instead, take a good, long look at the way you are directing it. If you are not too happy with the results, change them. Forget the past; there is nothing you can do about that. Forget about the real or imagined injuries to your pride. Wipe the slate clean and start all over again. Build the kind of story that suits you—the role you will enjoy playing.

Act your part with honor.

EPICTETUS

All the world's a stage, and all the men and women in it merely players. They have their exits and their entrances; and one man in his time plays many parts.

SHAKESPEARE

Some say what's the salvation of
the movies. I say, run 'em backwards.
It can't hurt 'em and it's worth a trial.

WILL ROGERS

Purposefulness

How to Stay Healthy

Søren Kierkegaard, a Danish philosopher, once stated that despair means not being oneself. He pointed out that nothing can make a person sick sooner than feeling useless, unwanted, unchallenged, and unneeded, or feeling that the values other men pursue are empty and joyless for him. This is what happens to many men who retire from work at sixty-five and die soon thereafter.

I think we need to point out to people who are secretly bored or unhappy that they can live wonderfully long, productive lives if they will take the trouble to find themselves and what it is they really want. If they can find a purpose, it can fill them with new vitality. It will seem as though they have found the fountain of youth—the way to turn back time and live days filled with interest, excitement, and fulfillment.

I have met many people who found excitement and youth all their lives, and I am sure you have too. I remember interviewing the inventor of the bulldozer, Mr. LeTourneau, who built the giant earth-moving machines when everyone said it could not be done. People like him never age. Their minds and interests remain as young and healthy at eighty as they were at twenty. They have a high degree of empathy with others. They eat and sleep well; they work, play and love with gusto, and they have an almost impregnable resistance to illness.

A distinguished research man in this field, Dr. Sydney M. Jouard of the University of Florida, has said: "In thinking about health, I like to conjure up the image of a family of germs looking for a home in which they might multiply and flourish. If I were the leader of such a group, and had the well-being of my family at heart, I would avoid any man like the plague, as long as he was productively and enjoyably engaged in living and loving. I would wait until he lost hope, or became discouraged, or became ground down by the requirements of respectable role-playing. At that precise moment, I would invade; his body would then become as fertile a life-space for my breed of germs as a well-manured flower bed is for the geranium or the weed."

This is something to think about. You don't have to build bulldozers to be productively and enjoyably engaged in living and loving. But you do need a powerful purpose, a real reason for getting out of bed in the morning, something toward which you are working.

This is why people with settled purposes, people who know who they are and where they are going, actually achieve their goals. There is just no stopping them. They are filled with energy, drive, and purpose, and with too much good health to even slow down. You will find no cynicism in them, no suspicion of others, and no worrying about what other people will think. They are much too busy to fool with such nonsense. Are you one of these people? You can be.

The world belongs to the energetic.

EMERSON

The belief that youth is the happiest
time of life is founded on a fallacy.
The happiest person is the person who thinks
the most interesting thoughts . . .

WILLIAM LYON PHELPS

A sound mind in a sound body; if the former
be the glory of the latter, the latter
is indispensable to the former.

TRYON EDWARDS

Creative thinking

How to Solve a Problem

Have you ever encountered a sentence or paragraph that seemed to jump out of the page and hit you right between the eyes? It happens to me all the time. I have made a collection of sentences that have affected me that way, at least long enough to make me do some serious thinking.

Here is one I ran across the other day that stopped me. There is nothing particularly unusual about it. Maybe it will not affect you at all, but it did me. It was written by Professor Robert Seashore, Chairman of the Department of Psychology at Northwestern University: "The happiest people are not the people without problems; they are the people who know how to solve their problems."

People who seem to spend most of their time hanging onto the short end of the stick will tell you that it is because of their problems. I'm sure successful people have problems too, but instead of complaining about them, they solve them.

I wonder how many millions of people have sat and moped because they have problems they think are standing between them and the things they want. They don't realize that trouble distributes itself without favor all over the world. So it boils down not to a matter of problems but of people. And that's what it always comes back to.

There are several ways of trying to solve problems. One is the hectic or panic method. Some people want so frantically to solve their problem that they jump at any apparent escape-hole like birds knocking themselves out against a pane of glass. When one hole won't work, they try to find another. Sometimes they do, particularly if the problem is simple, but more often than not, it's actually the long way around. It generally results in a lot of wasted time, a lot of worry, and sleepless nights.

Experts claim that it is possible to learn a definite system of problem-solving that will fit most situations. Instead of jumping from one thing to another, think through each problem and its possible solutions before you do anything about it. There are six steps:

1. Define your problem clearly on paper.
2. List the obstacles standing in the way of your solving it.
3. List people or other idea sources that might help solve your problem.
4. List as many possible courses of action as you can think of, and take your time on this.
5. Try to visualize the results of each course of action.
6. Choose the course of action that seems best to you, and then pursue it. Stay with it long enough for it to work or to prove that it can't. If it finally doesn't, choose another.

This is the scientific way to solve problems.

Don't accept superficial solutions of difficult problems.

BERTRAND RUSSELL

The heart of all problems, whether economic, political, or social, is a human heart.

CHARLES EDWARDS

All problems become smaller if, instead of indulging them, you confront them. Touch a thistle timidly and it pricks you; grasp it boldly, and its spines crumble.

WILLIAM S. HALSEY

Self-confidence

The Feeling of Inferiority

A wise man once wrote: "To be human is to feel inferior." Did you know that there is probably not a human being alive who does not have feelings of inferiority? He may not be born with them, but he soon develops them.

Will Rogers said, "We're all ignorant, only about different things." It is also true that we are all inferior, in different ways. The person with a healthy, happy attitude toward his world recognizes his inferiorities as a normal part of being human. The neurotic or unbalanced person hates himself for his inferiorities; he feels that they represent weakness and abnormality when they really do nothing of the kind.

The well-adjusted person frankly admires others for their talents and abilities without feeling envious. In fact, he doesn't bring himself into comparison at all. He is happily resigned to the fact that he is not the best-looking, best-built, smartest, most talented, fastest, cleverest, funniest, most engaging person on earth.

Without even thinking about it, he seems to know that every person is a potpourri of strengths and weaknesses inherited from all his ancestors. No two of them were alike but each one had a slightly different strong point with the standard collection of weaknesses. None of us had a thing to say about who our parents were, and all the vehemence and prayer in the world is not going to do a thing about them. If we have knobby knees, or big feet, or an off-kilter figure, or have to wear glasses, or fail to cause people of the opposite sex to tear at our clothes as we walk down the street, or cannot do complicated mathematical problems in our heads, we still represent that which we have been given. The most intelligent and healthy thing we can do about it is to make best use of what we do have.

The experts say that each of us has deep reservoirs of ability—even genius—that we habitually fail to use. We fail to make use of our own private and individual talents because we are caught up in the absurd and impossible game of trying to be like other people who could no more be like us than we could be like them. We forget that other people feel inferior too.

Since there is no one else on earth just like us, how can we be inferior? We are, each of us, one of a kind, defying rigid comparison by any measuring stick. The next time you are in a room full of people, remember that every one of them feels inferior to some degree in many areas, just as you and I do. Consider your strong points and join the human race. Above all, concentrate on things which take your mind and your interest away from yourself. If you spend your life trying to match the strong points of others, you are doomed to a life of frustration and despair.

In all the affairs of life let it be your great care not to hurt your mind or offend your judgment. And this rule, if observed carefully in all your deportment, will be a mighty security to you in your undertakings.

EPICTETUS

Every man hath his proper gift of God, one after this manner, and another after that.

I CORINTHIANS 5:7

I think I have learned, in some degree at least, to disregard the old maxim "Do not get others to do what you can do yourself." My motto on the other hand is "Do not do that which others can do as well."

BOOKER T. WASHINGTON

Communication

The $40,000 Difference

Someone once asked the question, "What's the difference between a fifty-thousand-dollar-a-year executive and a ten-thousand-dollar-a-year executive?" Do you know the answer?

We know that the fifty-thousand-dollar-a-year man is not five times smarter than one earning ten thousand dollars a year.

We also know he doesn't put in five times as

many hours on the job. O.K., then, what's the difference, assuming they are at the same level of experience?

Let me give you the answer supplied by Howard Bradley Smith. He says the difference between the two men is their relative ability to communicate. The highly paid executive knows the value of time. The more people with whom he can effectively communicate, the better. You can say exactly the same thing, in the same length of time, to five hundred people that you can say to one. In the same period of time you have made yourself five hundred times as effective.

Mr. Smith also says that the great majority of aspiring executives, and many already at the top, would give anything if they could walk up those three short steps to the speaker's platform and make an effective speech. However, they do not understand that it is no more difficult to speak to five hundred people than it is to speak to one, or two, or three. Would you say that you can speak with ease to three people, but not to four? Or to forty, but not to fifty? It's really absurd, isn't it? Well then, what's the secret?

The big trouble is fear. The next problem is really knowing your subject. People sometimes feel they don't have to be particularly prepared to talk to two or three people, but that's not true if a person aspires to become a fifty-thousand-dollar-a-year executive.

If a man wants to be able to get on his feet and talk to two hundred or five hundred people, the first thing he has to do is know his subject thoroughly. He should then prepare his speech so carefully, jam it with so much real meat, that he gets excited about it—that he actually wants to tell someone about it. Then he should remember that he has to forget himself and think of the good he can do for his audience. They need the information he has or he would not be talking to them in the first place. They want to hear what he has to say. Then, too, with a large group of people he has a tremendous extra factor going for him: mass enthusiasm. He should talk on one subject, enliven it with interesting stories, examples that prove his point—not jokes, but human interest cases to drive home his ideas. Finally, he should summarize what he has talked about, and then very graciously thank his listeners for listening to him. And that is it! That's often the difference between the ten-thousand- and the fifty-thousand-dollar-a-year man.

Wise men talk because they have something to say; fools because they would like to say something.

PLATO

Let your speech be always with grace, seasoned with salt, that ye may know how ye ought to answer every man.

COLOSSIANS 6:6

There are three things to aim at in public speaking; first to get into your subject, then to get your subject into yourself, and lastly, to get your subject into your hearers.

ALEXANDER GREGG

Criticism

No Matter How It Hurts

I understand there is a religious order of some kind which considers it an aspect of Christian love to be absolutely honest with each other, no matter how it hurts. For example, if one of their number is a teacher, and he tends to mumble instead of speaking distinctly, they consider it their brotherly duty to tell him about it. It is considered to be unloving to let a person go on making the same mistake forever just because one doesn't have love and courage enough to take the chance of hurting him, or of retaliation on his part.

Dr. Abraham H. Maslow, of the Department of Psychology of Brandeis University, says: "The person who is criticized honestly may be hurt for the moment but ultimately he is helped thereby and cannot but become grateful. Anyway, it is a great sign of respect to me, for instance, if someone feels I'm strong enough and capable enough and objective enough so that he can tell me where I have pulled a boner. It is only those people who regard me as delicate, sensitive, weak, or fragile who will not dare to disagree with me."

How do you feel about this? I think Dr. Maslow is right. At a dinner party I attended some time back, the very attractive woman seated next to me had managed, in wrestling with corn-on-the-cob, to get some of her lipstick on her chin. I immediately noticed it, and since I didn't know her well, debated with myself for a moment as to whether I should tell her about it. I had the feeling no one else would, at least not for some time, and felt that her embarrassment would be much greater later. So I quietly whispered the news to her. She removed the offending smear from her chin and thanked me for bringing it to her attention. She said exactly what I thought she would, that she would have been terribly embarrassed to find it later and realize she had appeared ridiculous to a great number of people for so long a time.

The wise person will tell others quite freely

and without dishonesty that he is glad that they did such-and-such, or that that was a nice thing to do, or that you made him sad and disappointed, etc. People, and especially children, then know where they stand. Disappointments and frustrations are not allowed to build up in a pocket of the mind where they can become swollen and fester.

A man will criticize his wife for burning the toast, but how often does he compliment her on the good meals? Like Dr. Maslow, I think it is unloving to let a person go on making the same mistake. I also feel we have an equal responsibility to openly praise, or at least recognize success and achievement.

The secret test to which criticism should be put before it is spoken is to make sure it is born of love and courage—not out of anger, or spite, or a desire to make the other person feel small.

Censure and criticism never hurt anybody.
If false, they can't hurt you unless you are
wanting in manly character; and if true, they
show a man his weak points, and forewarn him
against failure and trouble.

GLADSTONE

Honest criticism and sensitive
appreciation are directed not upon
the poet but upon the poetry.

T. S. ELIOT

Honesty

The Unfailing Boomerang

Certainly one of the most amazing, distressing, confounding, and resolute integrants of a human being is his adamant refusal to learn from experience—whether it be his own or the experience of others. If there is one great and unchanging law that he likes best to break, much to his own discomfort, pain, and amazement, it is the one I call "The Unfailing Boomerang."

Let me explain. Just about anybody you ask will tell you that truth is a great thing. Wonderful! Honesty? Great! The Golden Rule? A great piece of inspirational philosophy! So far, so good.

Yet I would be willing to bet my best hat that not one out of ten people you talk with in the course of your daily life understands the "reaction" to untruthfulness and dishonesty. Here is where the unfailing boomerang comes into the picture. Action—reaction. This is what makes the world go around.

Every time a person does something dishonest, he is, in effect, tossing a boomerang. How far out it will travel, no one knows. How great or how small a circle it will traverse, only time will tell. But it will, eventually it must, finally come swift and unseen around behind that person and deliver its never-failing and painful blow to the back of his neck. The same principle holds when a person conducts himself in a truthful and honest fashion. Good results from good acts are just as certain as bad results from bad acts. Each act is an unfailing boomerang.

We are all familiar with the famous biblical passage, "As ye sow, so shall ye reap." But I think we would all be surprised at the number of human beings who fail to realize that this law of the boomerang applies to everything we do every day of our lives, in business and away from business, with every person with whom we come in contact. It is so simple, so logical, so right, and so thoroughly misunderstood.

You would think, after thousands of years of human development, we would take this law as much for granted as we do food, drink, sleep, and breathing. But it seems that slowly, painfully, through trial and error, almost every member of each new generation has to learn it all over again, or suffer the consequences. The trick, it seems to me, is to get our youngsters to think in terms of action and reaction. Good action, good reaction; bad action, and bad reaction.

A life, a marriage, or a business without a foundation of honesty must fail in time. They are built on sand, and the higher they go, the farther they are going to fall, eventually.

The dishonest person is his own worst enemy, and while he can create a lot of mischief in the world, he is, in the end, his own victim. The tougher things get, the more frantically he begins to look for ways out. Since he is running on the wrong track, his problems compound themselves. Unless he wakes up to the fact that he has brought his trouble upon himself by his past actions and does a fast right-about-face, he has had it! Without question, he and others like him are the most frustrated, confused, bitter, disillusioned, and demoralized people on the face of the earth.

As a guideline in the face of an important decision, ask yourself, "Is this right?"; "Is this the honest thing to do?" And especially: "What is the *reaction* going to be?"

Joseph Parker wrote: "Falsehood is in a hurry; it may be at any moment detected and punished; truth is calm, serene; its judgment is on high; its king cometh out of the chambers of eternity."

He that buildeth a fair house upon an ill seat, committeth himself to prison.

FRANCIS BACON

To most men, experience is like the stern lights of a ship, which illuminate only the track it has passed.

SAMUEL TAYLOR COLERIDGE

Has any man ever attained to inner harmony by pondering the experience of others? Not since the world began! He must pass through the fire.

NORMAN DOUGLAS

Friendship

The Magic Marble

My old friend Fred Smith from Cincinnati told me an interesting story about a friend of his who always holds a marble in his hand whenever he talks with someone. Fred noticed that early in any conversation the man would reach into his pocket and out would come the marble which he would hold during the chat. Fred asked him about it, remarking that it reminded him of Captain Queeg's ball bearings in The Caine Mutiny.

His friend laughed. "This is my magic marble, Fred. Years ago, I had a hard time getting along with people. I knew a great many people, but actually had very few friends. One day I was talking with one of these friends when I noticed his attention was wandering. I was talking but he was looking out the window, his thoughts a million miles away.

"Later, I got to thinking about it and made a very embarrassing discovery. I realized that I had been talking about myself, that I *always* did. Conversations with others were really nothing more than opportunities to talk about what *I* was doing, what *I* thought, what *I* wanted. When others were talking, I wasn't thinking much about what they were saying; I was reloading to tell them all about myself. It dawned on me why I had so few friends. I wasn't *being* a friend. I wasn't interested in what was happening to others and what they thought at all.

"So, I made up my mind to change. I resolved to become interested in others, to let them do the talking, to steer the conversation back to them and their ideas. It's difficult to break a habit of years, but I found the solution the day I dropped into a five and dime and bought this marble. I call the marble 'Importance' and I make sure it's always on the side of the other person. I have never had a problem with people since. That little marble has made hundreds of friends for me. It has also taught me to quit thinking about myself all the time. I've found myself becoming genuinely interested in others. When that happens, you make friends in a hurry."

Well, that is the story of the magic marble. When I heard it, it made me think, long and soberly, about my own conduct in conversations. I asked myself if I had been tossing the ball to the other person or trying to hog the conversation with regard to my own interests. I wasn't sure, so I started making sure.

The thing to remember is that other people are far more interested in themselves than they are in you. You accomplish nothing by talking about yourself; but you accomplish a great deal by showing interest in what the other person is saying and doing. You make him feel that he or she is important in your eyes, and whenever you do this well, you might call it "instant friendship." It works like a charm every time.

Those who have the largest hearts have the soundest understandings; and he is the truest philosopher who can forget himself.

WILLIAM HAZLITT

Self-interest is but the survival of the animal in us.

FRÉDÉRIC AMIEL

If a man is worth knowing at all, he is worth knowing well.

ALEXANDER SMITH

202

Self-improvement

Every Man Is Two Men

Every man, in reality, is two men.

He is the man who leaves home at about the same time every morning to go to work. He is the man who has achieved a level of performance at his work sufficient to draw his pay, earn an occasional raise, and even a promotion from time to time. He and his work are satisfactory. He has, perhaps unconsciously, patterned his work habits after those with whom he works. He uses them as his bench marks for success, and they, in turn, are—again, perhaps unconsciously—using him for the same measurement. This is the man his employer, his family, and he himself know.

But he is also another man. He is the man he could be. Strongly motivated and equipped with the right sort of information, he could narrow the gap between his habitual performance patterns and his own much higher potential.

To visualize this, get a mental picture of a man standing inside the outline of a considerably larger man. Let this outline represent his highest potential. Of course, no one can say just how large the gap is between present performance and potential. It is, undoubtedly, different with each of us. There are some men who have grown, through constant study and self-examination and the application of their talents and abilities, to a pretty close approximation of their real potential. But I am of the opinion that these exceptional men represent an infinitesimal minority.

In most of us there is a sizable area for development. The greatest profit potential, to the employer as well as the employee, lies in this kind of personal development.

The development of people, whether directed by someone else or by the people themselves, should be a never-ending process. To the well-managed company this should be as important as its advertising; for here is profit that can be increased without plant expansion or capital investment. In terms of results that can be measured and tabulated, the cost is ridiculously low. It is, in fact, the best investment a company can make.

However, this is not, by any stretch of the imagination, exploitation or manipulation of human beings. They themselves benefit as much as or more than the employer. By exposing them to the kind of information that helps them develop as persons, we help them reach into their deep reservoirs of ability and bring more of it to the surface. We help them become not just better thinkers and producers, but better human beings in every way. We help them find a new awareness, a new joy and excitement in living.

To motivate human beings is not to force feed them or attempt to inflict our ideas upon them. They are at all times free to reject or ignore that to which they are exposed. But they usually do not.

Yes, every person is, in reality, two persons. He is the person he is today and he is the person he can be tomorrow. There is an exciting and rewarding area of development awaiting each of us!

True contentment is the power of getting out of any situation all that there is in it.

G. K. CHESTERTON

Every person is responsible for all the good within the scope of his abilities; and for no more, and none can tell whose sphere is the largest.

GAIL HAMILTON

The indefatigable pursuit of an unattainable

perfection, even though it consists in nothing more than in the pounding of an old piano, is what alone gives a meaning to our life on this unavailing star.

LOGAN PEARSALL SMITH

Adversity

What Makes Us Tick?

A major part of this book is about what makes people tick and how so many of us could do a lot better if we would direct more of our thinking and energy toward higher purposes. Of course there are lower, downright nefarious purposes, too.

Alex Osborn reminded me of this recently with a story of amazing human ingenuity pointed in the wrong direction.

Osborn's story is about a man who had been something of a good-for-nothing floater. His wife finally got fed up with him and threw him out. For years, he had been sitting around doing nothing, letting his wife support him. It wasn't until she rejected him that he suddenly became extremely active and inventive. His hatred then led him to invent a machine to kill her.

Time magazine described the device he made as "a package camera ingeniously devised of cream cheese boxes, wire, and an empty tin can with an innocent baked bean label. This casting concealed a twelve-gauge single-shot, sawed-off shotgun." With fiendish cleverness, the man picked up a strange girl and persuaded her to find his first wife and "snap a picture of her" with that lethal camera. He told her he was a detective and that his quarry was a jewel thief. The empty-headed girl had no idea she was carrying around an infernal machine until she innocently shot off the wife's leg with that so-called camera.

Consider the imagination this man displayed. If he had used the same ingenuity and relentless singleness of purpose to a good end a few years sooner, if he had simply employed his creative mind along constructive lines, he wouldn't have had a problem in the world.

Each of us is motivated by many things. Andrew Carnegie once began an address to a student body by saying, "I address myself only to those among you who have ambition to become millionaires." Greed for gold provides an emotional drive in many pursuits, including the creative. But as W. B. Wiegand put it, "The motive power which stokes the fires of creative thought is far more subtle and, indeed, far more potent than the lure of gold. It is ofttimes a spirit of intellectual adventure will supply this magic touch of motivation." Yes, men and women *are* motivated by the desire for more money, more things, higher status, keeping up with the Joneses. But they are also motivated by the spirit of intellectual adventure. We are motivated by vanity, which we hide under the term "self-realization."

The dread of poverty, as Alex Osborn points out in his book *Applied Imagination*, is an even stronger urge than the hope of riches. This fact makes adversity an ally of creative effort. In fact, adversity is often the best thing that can happen to a person. It stimulates him to greater effort and can lead him into areas he never would have known and enjoyed. Often, things we begin out of sheer necessity come with time to be our most interesting and rewarding pursuits. In almost every case of adversity there is the seed of a great hope.

> *The art of living is more like that of wrestling than of dancing; the main thing is to stand firm and be ready for an unforeseen attack.*
>
> MARCUS AURELIUS

> *Sweet are the uses of adversity.*
>
> SHAKESPEARE

> *When fate is adverse, a wise man can always strive fror happiness and sail against the wind to attain it.*
>
> ROUSSEAU

Kindness

It Makes a Difference

Some time ago, I met a man—let's call him John—who had been an artillery officer in World War II. John began to tell me how his battalion came very close to being overrun during the Battle of the Bulge. He and his men managed to hold their position but were exposed to the cold for such a long period that John's feet were frozen.

The battalion doctor told John that he should send him back for hospitalization. But the doctor was afraid that, because of the sudden great surge of injured flooding back from the front, the rear echelon surgeons might amputate John's feet. The doctor suggested that John stay where he was and, while he could not promise anything, he would try his best to save his feet.

As it turned out, the doctor was able to do just that. Today, the Battle of the Bulge and the frozen feet are only a memory. But a big part of that memory is of a doctor who went to a lot of special trouble despite his crowded, hectic days.

We can all look back to someone who took special pains to help us. In many cases, it was a conscientious parent or teacher who refused to be satisfied with merely doing his or her job and no more. I think there is a lesson here for all of us: what we do is important. We should never get the feeling that what we do is not important and therefore take the easy or expedient way out of a situation.

You can never tell when something you might say or do, just a little extra effort on your part, might go a long way toward helping someone. That person will remember you and your action, or your words, for many years to come. He may even pick up the baton of helpfulness and pass it along to someone else.

You don't have to wait for large and important occasions to be helpful. The opportunity is present every day. Just as we have been helped by thoughtful and conscientious people ourselves, we will do well to remember that a word, an act of kindness, or some generosity can make a big difference in someone's life. And that someone may be numbered among your children, your friends and associates, your neighbors, or even passing strangers.

Every day of your life is filled with opportunities to be larger instead of smaller; polite and thoughtful, instead of rude or careless; to love a little more and hate a little less. By these small acts you will improve your image in the minds of others. By your actions you will be teaching—and demonstrating to your world that you are mature enough to take the initiative in being helpful, rather than just doing the least you can.

As with anything else, the best place to start is where you are right now. Of one thing you can be certain, you will never be sorry for having been kind. It is the times when you are unkind that you will remember with shame. Do not ever say, "What I do doesn't really matter." It does. Wordsworth wrote: "The best portion of a good man's life is his little, nameless, unremembered acts of kindness and of love.

Kindness is the golden chain by which society is bound together.

GOETHE

The smallest effort is not lost
Each wavelet on the ocean tost

Aids in the ebb-tide or the flow;
Each rain-drop makes some floweret blow;
Each struggle lessens human woe.

Charles Mackay

Praise

The Climate for Growth

One day several years ago I stopped my car for gas at a service station in Hollywood, California. While the middle-aged owner of the station cheerfully went about taking care of my car's needs, I noticed that while the station was by no means new, it was spotlessly clean. I was particularly amazed by the driveway; it was as clean as if my car were the first to use it.

I asked the owner how in the world he managed to keep the driveway spotless with dozens of cars dripping oil and tracking the dirt of the highways on it. He told me how a common product, sold in every supermarket, was in his estimation the best driveway cleaner in the world. He beamed in response to my comment on the way he kept his place of business. It was a valuable moment for both of us: I learned something of value, and he experienced the pleasure of honest praise.

The need for praise is basic to everyone. With it, a person blooms and grows. Without it, he tends to shrink and withdraw into himself.

I remember reading about a woman who left a dozen jars of homemade jelly on the kitchen counter top for several weeks. Finally, she asked her husband to carry them down to the basement. It was only then that he noticed the work she had done and complimented her on it.

We all know children need constant praise and encouragement. When a child brings home a piece of art work that looks for all the world like an unfortunate accident, he still expects an encouraging word. But his need for encouragement is no less than his mother's and father's. Far too many mothers and fathers aren't getting any praise, or at least not nearly enough.

Understanding the importance of self-esteem and seeing the never-ending need for reaffirmation of a person's worth, we should make it our business to watch for honest opportunities to give praise—especially to the members of our families and those with whom we work. There is a subtle but enormously valuable by-product of backfire to this sort of thing: In order to praise others, we need to look for the good. It forces us to concentrate on what's right with people and the things they do, rather than on what's wrong. It focuses our attention on the positive side of the ledger and, as a result, makes us happier, more productive, and more pleasant to be around. Then, too, people like those who praise them and recognize their value. When we give praise we attract a larger circle of friends. And finally, giving praise is the best known way to receive it. It's hard for anyone to compliment a chronic grouch.

Whenever you hear someone say, "Nobody appreciates me . . . nobody gives me credit for all I do," the chances are he is so wrapped up in himself and in getting happiness from others, he has completely forgotten how to give.

We should try to find some way to commend those we love every day. Praise to a human being represents what sunlight, water, and soil are to a plant; the climate in which he grows best. He does not just want it, he needs it as he needs the air he breathes.

One good deed dying tongueless slaughters a thousand waiting upon that. Our praises are our wages.

SHAKESPEARE

The most agreeable recompense which we can receive for things which we have done is to see them known, to have them applauded with praises which honor us.

MOLIÈRE

There can hardly, I believe, be imagined a more desirable pleasure than that of praise unmixed with any possibility of flattery.

STEELE

217

Success

A Day at a Time

One of the surprising anachronisms of our age is that the great majority of people still think of success as a matter of luck, getting the breaks, being born rich, or being crooked. It is not, nor has it ever been, any of these things. The formula for success is known, and it is as simple as adding two and two. But you will have a hard time convincing some people of this—namely those who still cling to their old wives' tales and who alibi their own failures by perpetuating such nonsense.

Here is a formula for success which will work every time, for any man or woman. A lifetime consists of years, months, weeks, and days. The basic unit of a lifetime is a single day. And a single day in our careers is made up of certain acts which each of us must perform.

We need only perform successfully each act of a single day to enjoy a successful day. Repeat this each day for a week, and you have a successful week. If you will only do each day the things you know you should do each day and do them as successfully as you possibly can, you can rest assured that you will be successful all the years of your life. You don't have to run around in circles trying to do a great many things. It is not the number of acts you perform but rather the efficacy with which you perform them that counts. Don't try to do do tomorrow's or next week's work today. Just do today's as best you can and leave tomorrow's for tomorrow. That is really all there is to it.

The country is full of successful people who don't even know they are successful. And it is also full of unsuccessful people who think they are successful. The important thing is not to slight a single act during the day, because sometimes we do not know how really important some little act may be. The minute one rises in the morning, he is faced with certain things to do. He should be cheerful, for example, to the other members of his family. A person has the choice of being cheerful or sad. With these two alternatives, no one with any sense or understanding of life would choose to be unhappy. Then there is our work.

Have you ever thought how boring and uneventful life would be without our work? Here again, work consists of a series of things to do. We have only to perform each one as best we can to be successful all day long. Finally, if we can go to bed again in the comforting knowledge that we have done the best we could do for that one day, we can know that we are successful. As Emerson put it: "Self-trust is the first secret of success, the belief that if you are here the authorities of the universe put you here, and for cause."

Your job, then, is to play out the role you have undertaken to the best of your ability. Success is nothing more nor less than this. We only become dull and bored and uneasy with ourselves and others when we shirk what we know full well we should be doing. The happiest and most contented people are those who each day perform to the best of their ability.

The truth about success is long overdue. There is nothing mysterious about it. Success can be predicted and measured with mathematical precision and will come to us in the exact degree of the effectiveness with which we live each day.

Concentration is my motto—first honesty, then industry, then concentration.

CARNEGIE

I never did anything worth doing by accident, nor did any of my inventions come by accident.

EDISON

The man who does not work for the love of work, but only for money is neither likely to make money nor to find much fun in life.

CHARLES M. SCHWAB

Self-discipline

What Failures Won't Do

In a speech delivered a long time ago, Albert E. N. Gray talked about the few who succeed in a world where success is available to everyone.

He pointed out that if you would succeed, you must form the habit of doing the things that failures don't like to do. "Success is something achieved by the minority of men," he said, "and it is therefore unnatural and not to be achieved by following our natural likes and dislikes, nor by being guided by our natural preferences and prejudices."

So then, successful men have formed the habit of doing the things that failures don't like to do. Why? Because they have found this is the only way to achieve their goals. Successful men are influenced by the desire for pleasing results. Failures are influenced by the desire for pleasing methods, less concerned with results.

Why are successful men able to do things the failures won't do? Because successful men have a purpose strong enough to make them form the habit of doing these things.

There you have it. It is one of the simplest and best reasons why a small minority is successful, while the majority seems to be satisfied with average results. And it all boils down to purpose, doesn't it?

Successful men are influenced by the desire for pleasing *results.* Failures are willing to accept poor or mediocre results so long as what they do to achieve them is comfortable and pleasant.

The man from whom I obtained a copy of Gray's speech is a top executive in one of the country's largest businesses. He told me his life was completely changed after hearing that speech in Philadelphia back in 1940. He resolved to make a habit of doing what the failures don't like to do. Once it became second nature to him, his outstanding achievements followed.

You might ask, "But is it worth it?" To my mind it is. I have always felt that life is too short, too precious, to let it slip away while we vegetate. There will be plenty of time for rest later—all the time there is. Besides, who enjoys his rest and leisure better than the person who does his work the best he can, to the limit of his abilities?

Success is something achieved by the minority of men, and it is therefore unnatural. It is extraordinary. It can be achieved only by extraordinary methods.

*Who reigns within himself, and
rules passions, desires, and fears
is more than a king.*

MILTON

*This is a world of action, not
for droning in.*

DICKENS

*Fortunate is the person who has developed
the self-control to steer a straight course
toward his objective. . . .*

NAPOLEON HILL

*I guess more players lick themselves
than are ever licked by an opposing team.
The first thing any man has to know
is how to handle himself.*

CONNIE MACK

Excellence

How to Succeed Like Nobody's Business

Some time ago, a telephone company ran a series of ads on the Quest for Excellence. I enjoyed them and I think they represented a type of advertising that should be adopted by more companies and associations. Listen to this ad—it is titled "You Can Feel It in Your Bones!"

The feeling for quality, the instinct for excellent performance, can get into your very bones. Quality can *make* work worth doing.

And the feeling for quality, once it *does* get into your bones, can be a terrific asset. It can give dignity to the individual. It can give character to the business. It can give satisfaction to customers.

Your personal "quest for excellence" can be another way of saying "my character is showing." And the character of this business is nothing more nor less than the sum total of the characters of the *people* in the business. So long as we seek excellence, and accept nothing less, our business will succeed like nobody's business!

That's good, isn't it? I don't see how anybody can read something like that and not try a little harder for excellence in his life and work. I particularly like the lines "The feeling for quality, the instinct for excellent performance, can get into your very bones. Quality can make work worth doing." And it can. It can give meaning and richness to a human life.

In business, the constant and never-ending search for quality should be paramount. People are naturally attracted to quality. It is something everyone wants; it is what we all aspire to. It is what a man wants in his car, his home, and everything he buys. The people who demand excellence in the product they manufacture or the service they provide will prevail. They will always come out on top.

Any person who produces less than his very best is cheating. And, as Emerson was fond of pointing out, in the long haul he cheats only himself.

In Ernest Hemingway's book *A Moveable Feast,* he tells of the early days of his striving, when he and his wife were poor as church mice, living over a sawmill in Paris. Every day he would go to the room where he worked and labor over his writing. Sometimes he would spend an entire morning working on a single paragraph. It had to be right, as right as he could make it, or he would tear it up. When he finally received the Nobel Prize for Literature as well as the acclaim of the world and the rich rewards of success, it was because of his insistence upon excellence during all the years that had gone before.

Every year, thousands of businesses fail, hundreds of thousands of men and women are discharged from their jobs, because they tried to get maximum results from minimum effort. It used to be that when men parted they would say, "Work hard." Today, it is "Take it easy." How often have you heard the expression "I'm not going to knock myself out; I do no more than I have to." It seems to me that people with that philosophy are the poorest people on earth.

The quest for excellence gives dignity to a person. It gives character to a business. It gives satisfaction to customers. So long as we seek excellence and accept nothing less, our business *will* succeed like nobody's business.

(*We are what we repeatedly do. Excellence, then, is not an act but a habit.*)

ARISTOTLE

Each honest calling, each walk of life, has its own aristocracy based on excellence of performance.

JAMES BRYANT CONANT

In business, excellence of performance manifests itself, among other things, in the advancing of methods and processes; in the improvement of products; in more perfect organization, eliminating friction as well as waste; in bettering the condition of the working men, developing their faculties and promoting their happiness; and in the establishment of right relations with customers and with the community.

LOUIS D. BRANDEIS

Maturity and initiative

Thoughts of Value

Harry Emerson Fosdick once wrote: "The great day comes when a man begins to get himself off his hands. He has lived, let us say, in a mind like a room surrounded by mirrors. Every way he turned he saw himself. Now, however, some of the mirrors change to windows. He can see through them to objective outlooks that challenge his interests. He begins to get out of himself, no longer the prisoner of self-reflections but a free man in a world where persons, causes, truths, and values exist, of value for their own sakes. Thus to pass from a mirror-mind to a mind with windows is an essential step in the development of real personality. Without that experience no one ever achieves a meaningful life."

This is a good rule-of-thumb to determine whether or not your life is meaningful. Just ask yourself, and answer honestly, whether or not yours is a room of mirrors or of windows. There are certain to be some mirrors, I suppose, but the relation of mirrors to windows can give you an idea of your degree of maturity and real happiness.

It is a good simile because it gives us a chance to think about life in a new way—as a room. No one could long be happy living in a room of mirrors with all the world shut out. But with even one window, you could see some of the world outside, and as you grow and mature as a person, you open more windows until finally, and ideally, the walls have disappeared and you are one with the world.

Here is another quotation I like, from Lansing P. Shield: "Research in the minds of men will parallel research in the field of mechanics. The machine has carried us far; men will carry us farther and faster.

"Our American system is still in its infancy; we scarcely have scratched the surface of a deep deposit of initiative; we have but tapped the resources of the free enterprise system. The initiative of a mere minority has yielded unparalleled results. What tremendous horizons loom if we fully develop the initiative of the majority! The limits of our American way are only those vast expanses of about two hundred million creative minds, two hundred million creative minds in which the spark of individual initiative awaits only release. Machines move mountains, but initiative moves men."

It is important that each of us remembers that word "initiative." To the extent that initiative is reduced in our country will our progress as a nation be slowed. Conversely, if we can maintain and improve the rewards which trigger initiative, we will become progressively stronger, healthier, and richer as a people. Initiative is to a man what fuel is to a rocket; the more you have, the higher and farther you can travel.

People without initiative are people without hope. If you find your initiative in short supply, maybe it is because you have not decided where you want to go and what you want to do.

Carlyle wrote: "Show me the man you honor, and I will know what kind of man you are, for it shows me what your ideal of manhood is, and what kind of a man you long to be."

When everything has its proper place in our minds, we are able to stand in equilibrium with the rest of the world.

FRÉDÉRIC AMIEL

Man is preeminently a creative animal, predestined to strive consciously for an object and to engage in engineering—that is, incessantly and eternally to make new roads, wherever they may lead.

FEODOR DOSTOEVSKI

If I had the opportunity to say a final word to all the young people in America, it would be this: Don't think too much about yourself.

CHARLES W. ELIOT

Using time wisely

The Big Difference

One of my favorite stories was told to me some years back by a university professor. While he and his wife were visiting a city in India, he had noticed a Hindu who did nothing but sit by the river. Every time he looked the man would be sitting there.

One day the professor's curiosity got the better of him and, ostensibly taking a walk, he spoke to the Hindu. To his surprise the man answered him in excellent English. When asked why he seemed to spend all of his time in such a manner, the Hindu replied that he believed in reincarnation. According to his belief we have all lived many times before and will live many times again. And then he said, "This life I'm sitting out."

From that extreme to handling a job such as President of the United States, or of one of our larger corporations, it can be said that what happens to a person during his lifetime is in direct relation to the way he passes his days.

To my way of thinking, we should be concerned about two periods of time, the present and the future. Although no one person can be absolutely certain that a future exists for him, he is wise to plan for it. Some people, it is true, overdo this and concentrate so strongly on the future that they forget to live fully in the present.

Millions more, I am sure, are so preoccupied with today or tomorrow that they fail to plan at all beyond the present. Then, of course, there are those who neither plan for the future nor enjoy the present. They are people who seem to lack a consciousness of living.

Only a few people spend their time wisely, enjoying each day, yet preparing themselves for a pleasant and comfortable future. Are you one of these fortunate few?

I remember a Russian author's story about a young man who was to be executed for murder.

As dawn broke, the young man stood at the window of his prison cell where he could see over the walls to the countryside beyond. It was summer, and at the first light of the beautiful day, a change came over the young man.

Suddenly he became tremendously interested in seeing the first, faint rays of the sun touch the leaves of the trees; he noticed the rich, brown earth and the bright green of the fields. As he gripped the bars of his cell and stared intently at the scene which had been played every morning for countless centuries, tears started down his cheeks. He realized that he was seeing the true glory and the magnificence of the world for the first time in his life.

As the jailers arrived to take him to the place of execution, he was still transfixed by the unspeakable beauty of the sunrise. The wonder of life had been there all along. He had simply waited too long to begin enjoying it. And he was not alone in the world. Since our tomorrows will be unlike our todays, we need to try to visualize them and prepare. But we should be mindful also that life can waste itself while we are preparing to live.

> *Always hold fast to the present hour. Every state of duration, every second, is of infinite value . . . I have staked on the present as one stakes a large sum on one card, and I have sought without exaggerating to make it as high as possible.*
>
> GOETHE

Each man should frame life so that at some future hour fact and his dreamings meet.

VICTOR HUGO

To the being fully alive, the future is not ominous but a promise; it surrounds the present like a halo.

JOHN DEWEY

Youth

Who's the Delinquent?

Have you ever wondered what goes on in the mind of a juvenile delinquent? Do you really know your children? Do you ever have long talks with your youngsters . . . listen to their problems, hopes, plans?

I want to share with you a letter that moved me deeply. It was written by a boy with a record as a juvenile delinquent. He wrote it to his parents, who sent it to a Kansas City newspaper with a note reading: "Perhaps, if we share this letter through your newspaper, it will help other parents."

Dear Folks,

Thank you for everything, but I am going to Chicago and try and start some kind of new life.

You asked me why I did those things and why I gave you so much trouble, and the answer is easy for me to give you, but I am wondering if you will understand.

Remember when I was about six or seven and I used to want you to just listen to me? I remember all the nice things you gave me for Christmas and my birthday and I was really happy with the things—about a week—at the time I got the things, but the rest of the time I just wanted all the time for you to listen to me like I was somebody who felt things too, because I remember even when I was young I felt things. But you said you were busy.

Mom, you are a wonderful cook, and you had everything so clean and you were tired so much from doing all those things that made you busy; but, you know something, Mom? I would have liked crackers and peanut butter just as well—if you had only sat down with me a while during the day and said to me, "Tell me all about it so I can maybe help you understand."

And when Donna came and I couldn't understand why everyone made so much fuss because I didn't think it was my fault that her hair is curly and her skin so white, and she doesn't have to wear glasses with such thick lenses. Her grades were better, too, weren't they?

If Donna ever has children, I hope you will tell her to just pay some attention to the one who doesn't smile very much because that one will really be crying inside. And when she's about to bake six dozen cookies, to make sure first that the kids don't want to tell her about a dream or a hope or something, because thoughts are important too, to small kids even though they don't have so many words to use when they tell about what they have inside them.

I think that all the kids who are doing so many things that grown-ups are tearing out their hair worrying about are really looking for somebody that will have time to listen a few minutes and who really and truly will treat them as they would a grown-up who might be useful to them. You know—be polite to them. If you folks had ever said, "Pardon me," when you interrupted me, I'd have dropped dead!

If anybody asks you where I am, tell them I've gone looking for somebody with time because I've got a lot of things I want to talk about.

Love to All,

Your Son.

Yes, that's the letter of a boy with a police record.

How about taking the time to talk with your kids, listen to what's bothering them, find out what they think. Let them know they are important to you—let them know you love them and respect them as persons.

In the man whose childhood has known caresses and kindness, there is always a fibre of memory that can be touched to gentle issues.

GEORGE ELIOT

Children have more need of models than of critics.

JOSEPH JOUBERT

Family life is too intimate to be preserved by the spirit of justice. It can only be sustained by a spirit of love which goes beyond justice.

REINHOLD NIEBUHR

240

Energy

When You're Tired

Next time you get the chance, here is a little survey you can make. On any given morning, ask people how they feel. Particularly, ask secretaries, elevator operators, and others who work for wages, as opposed to homemakers who work, but don't get paid for it.

Maybe it is different in your town, but in mine the answer you will get about eighty-five per cent of the time is "I'm tired." Have you ever noticed how common this is?

And if the truth were known, it is a lot of nonsense! Do you know that you have deep, hidden reservoirs of power you may never have tapped?

Many years ago I discovered Professor William James's wonderful little book *On Vital Reserves.* In it he says that everyone knows what it is to start a piece of work, either intellectual or physical, feeling stale. And everyone knows what it is to warm up to his work. The process of warming up is particularly striking in the phenomenon known as "second wind." Now, usually, most people stop working at the first sign of fatigue. They say, "Boy, I'm bushed," and that's it for the day. As Dr. James put it, "We have then walked, played, or worked enough so therefore we desist." We simply quit. This sort of fatigue forms a kind of wall inside of which, as a rule, we work and live our lives.

But if an unusual necessity forces us to press onward, a surprising thing occurs. The fatigue gets worse up to a certain critical point, then gradually or suddenly it passes away and we are fresher than before. We have evidently tapped a level of new energy that had until then been masked by the "fatigue barrier" we usually obey. In fact, we may have discovered that we have third and fourth winds. This phenomenon occurs in mental activity as well as physical, and in some cases we may find, beyond the fatigue point, stores of energy that we never dreamed we possessed. Evidently, we stockpile reserves of energy we don't ordinarily use. And these reserves will only go to work when we demand enough of ourselves.

Only a few exceptional persons make any serious demands of themselves. The great majority of us miss the far greater accomplishments of which we are capable—and the greater joy in living this would bring to us—because we quit and sit down, gasping, at the first sign of fatigue. And I think this situation has been getting steadily worse.

I remember one Sunday when I knew I had to write ten radio shows, all in one day. I got started at nine o'clock in the morning, and by five o'clock that afternoon I was so bushed I could hardly think. But I still had five shows to write so I kept at it. All of a sudden I felt better and had more energy than I had previously . . . and by one-thirty the next morning when I finally finished, I felt great. Sixteen and one-half hours of steady mental work and I was fresh as a daisy! But I had felt like quitting after only seven or eight hours! The next time you get tired, keep at it and see what happens.

Each of us has a tremendous second wind, mental and physical. Passing through the fatigue barrier to draw upon our idle reserves can make the difference between existing and really living.

Experience shows that success is due less to ability than to zeal. The winner is he who gives himself to his work, body and soul.

BUXTON

Vigor is contagious; and whatever makes us either think or feel strongly adds to our power and enlarges our field of action.

EMERSON

Achievement

How to Get What You Want

A very wise man once said, "If you can tell me what you want, I can tell you how to get it." He was a wise man because he knew that the problem with people is not *their ability to achieve what they want. The great majority of people who are dissatisfied with their lives, who feel the world is passing them by and that they are not getting anywhere, are not suffering from a lack of ability. Far from it. They are suffering from not having decided where they want to go.*

William James, the father of American psychology, put it this way: "If you would be rich, you will be rich; if you would be good, you will be good; if you would be learned, you will be learned. Wish, then, for one thing exclusively and not for a hundred other incompatible things just as strongly."

So the secret to achievement is to decide on one thing you want very much. Yes, there are lots of other things you want too, but one thing at a time. Write down all the things you want and then pick the one, just one, that you want more than the rest. Stick with that one thing until it is achieved; then go on to the next item on your agenda.

A man following this course can accomplish more in five years than the average man accomplishes in forty. This is because the average man never seems to make the one decision that would give direction and purpose to his life.

A gentleman by the name of Bulwer put it this way: "The man who seeks one, and but one, thing in life may hope to achieve it; but he who seeks all things wherever he goes, only reaps, from the hopes which he sows, a harvest of barren regrets." This is the whole point. Seek one thing, not two or more . . . one thing at a time.

The next question: "How do I know I have the ability to achieve what I want?" The answer is that we do not seriously want things we don't have the ability to achieve. We all seem to have a built-in governor which keeps us from wanting things beyond our capabilities. That is why one man sets his heart on becoming a lawyer while another applies for a job with the forest service, or in an automobile factory. The wide spectrum of occupations and accomplishments shows us the diversity of human desires. Seeing a man working atop the dizzy heights of the steel skeleton of a skyscraper, you have probably said to yourself, "I wouldn't do that for all the money in the world." But he enjoys the work and will do it for so much an hour.

Have no doubt that you can accomplish your goal. It is deciding on the goal that can be the most crucial decision of your life. It has been written, "Providence has nothing good or high in store for one who does not resolutely aim at something high or good. A purpose is the eternal condition of success."

> *When a man has not a good reason for doing a thing, he has one good reason for letting it alone.*
>
> SCOTT

> *A man without decision can never be said to belong to himself; he is as a wave of the sea, or a feather in the air which every breeze blows about as it listeth.*
>
> FOSTER

Attitude

Xenophobia

What is your normal reaction toward strangers? Do you regard them with timidity, fear, hostility, or mistrust; or do you see them as potential friends until they prove themselves otherwise? Be honest now.

Or let me put it another way. Let us say you are a salesperson working in a large store. A customer walks up to you, someone you have never seen before. The customer might be a stout old lady, a teen-ager, or a man wearing work clothes; what is your attitude toward this stranger? Did you say

to yourself, "That depends upon his attitude toward me?"

There have been some fascinating studies made on this subject. Do you know that the great majority of people seem to react with distrust, even vague hostility, toward strangers? The reasons go back thousands of years to the time when people distrusted and even feared those they did not know because a traveler could be robbed and killed by a stranger. Spending the night in a wayside inn could result in having one's throat cut. Most hotel rooms to this day have formidable double or triple door locks with instructions to fasten the safety chain before retiring.

So, for many centuries the prudent person viewed strangers with either hostility or a good deal of caution and reserve. The Greeks had a word for this, xenophobia. Xeno means stranger and phobia means fear. Fear of strangers. As children we were taught to be wary of strangers, never to get into a stranger's car, or accept gifts from people we did not know.

I think that today, however, the mark of a mature adult is to treat strangers as friends. We don't live in the Dark Ages anymore. But have you noticed that most people wait to see how a stranger is going to act toward them before they show warmth or friendship, or for that matter, any feelings at all?

It seems most people are reactors—walking mirrors—who reflect to strangers exactly what the stranger projects. This is true, unfortunately, of thousands of salespeople. They permit others to decide for them how they are going to feel; whether they are going to be pleasant or unpleasant; warm or cool; polite or rude. But not the wise man. He decides for himself how he is going to feel, and he is not going to let others get him off the track. The wise man or woman knows that when he shows a warm, friendly attitude toward others, the majority will return it and the few who don't won't matter.

The greatest men in all ages have been lovers of their kind. All true leaders of men have it. Faith in men and regard for men are unfailing marks of true greatness.

EMERSON

Success or failure in business is caused more by mental attitude even than by mental capacities.

WALTER DILL SCOTT

I do not have to make over the universe;
I have only to do my job, great or small,
and look often at the trees and hills and sky,
and be friendly with all men.

DAVID GRAYSON

Education

The Fool in Us

A man by the name of M. J. Savage once wrote something that makes so much sense I would like to pass it along to you: "If any young man expects, without faith, without thought, without study, without patient, persevering labor, in the midst of and in spite of discouragement, to attain anything in this world that is worth attaining, he will simply wake up by-and-by and find that he has been playing the part of a fool."

Now that is a saying that should be emblazoned somewhere in every school, college and university in the land. It is something which I feel the young would be able to understand and believe. Frequently, young people—girls as well as boys—say, "Why should I work hard at my schoolwork? I don't know what I am going to do when I grow up." Or parents think it is not necessary for their daughter to get a good education since, as they so frequently put it, "She'll only get married and be a housewife anyway."

No matter what a person decides to do in his adult life, a solid educational background will help. And it will be just as valuable to the young woman as to the young man; it takes just as much education to be a successful wife and mother these days as it takes to succeed in business or the professions.

I am a firm believer in children enjoying themselves. But it is a little known fact that it is the best students who have the most fun. It is axiomatic that the people who do the least, whether they are seventeen or seventy, are the least happy. The griping, whining employee is always the one who turns in the worst job for his wages. He never learns that the more he tries to duck his work and still collect his pay, the more frustrated and miserable he will become.

The same thing holds true for youngsters. By taking the course of least resistance and trying to sneak by with minimal effort, they are only contributing to their own feelings of inadequacy. The extra, so-called "free" time this gives them only extends their boredom and deepens their frustration, whereas the conscientious student, confident and proud of his ability, enjoys his studies and savors all the more the free time he earns and can enjoy, since it has not been stolen at the cost of his future.

There never has been, there is not now, and there never will be a short road to success. The person who takes what he thinks to be the easy way will eventually, as Savage put it, "wake up by-and-by and find that he has been playing the part of a fool." How do you tell young people that their joy and happiness in life can never exceed the effort they put into their work?

All who have meditated on the art of governing mankind have been convinced that the fate of empires depends on the education of youth.

ARISTOTLE

Our greatest happiness . . . does not depend on the condition of life in which chance has placed us, but is always the result of a good conscience, good health, occupation and freedom in all just pursuits.

JEFFERSON

Creativity

How's Your Imagination?

Once upon a time a man took his girl on a picnic. It was a warm summer day and they had chosen as the picnic site a small island two miles from shore in a beautiful lake near their home. The man rowed his young ladylove to the island. At this point she decided, as a woman will, that she would like some ice cream. So the young man again climbed into the boat and began the four-mile round trip to shore and back.

As the perspiration began to stream down his face and his back and arms started

to ache, he pondered two things. The first was why a man permitted himself to be pushed around by a pretty girl. Finding no satisfactory answer to that age-old question, he turned his mind to why it was necessary to row a boat at all. He pictured himself sitting comfortably in the boat with the breeze blowing in his face and with a small motor propelling the boat for him.

Later he developed the outboard motor, married the pretty girl with the craving for ice cream, and earned a fortune. All because a four-mile, solitary row made him think. Big ships had motors and propellers, why not small boats?

When the Wright brothers invented the airplane, motors had already been invented; so had gliders. They put the two together and devised the airplane.

How is your creative imagination? Are you a curious observer? Do you ever play the creative game? Take any object; it can be a hairpin, a jackknife, a doorknob, anything at all. Ask yourself if it has to be the way it is. Stare at it; study it. Could it be different? Can it be improved? You don't have to be an inventor. This is just an exercise for improving your creative imagination. It can be applied to anything from raising kids to cooking better meals or making more money.

I remember reading an Oriental fable about a fabulously rich potentate who passed on, leaving all his possessions to his favorite slave, Yusef, with the exception that each of his sons should be allowed to pick one thing of value to have and hold forever. What would you have taken?

One son, the eldest, picked the royal palace; another, the great gardens; another, a lavishly jeweled throne of tremendous value; another selected a chest of precious gems. As each made his selection, his heart was sore that the remainder of the great estate would go to the slave. The elder sons were men of little imagination, as the story goes, because the youngest and last son to make his choice said, "I select for my possession, Yusef, the slave."

Training the mind to become more creative is a game any number can play at any time, anywhere. It can put new zest and interest into your work, more fun into your days. At dinner, you can play the game with the whole family taking part; just pick an object and ask why is it that way? How could it be improved?

The faculty of imagination is the great spring of human activity, and the principal source of human improvement. As it delights in presenting to the mind scenes and characters more perfect than those we are acquainted with, it prevents us from ever being completely satisfied with our present condition or with our past attainments and engages us in the pursuit of some untried method.

STEWART

Success

The First Law of Business

"Our rewards in life will always be in direct proportion to our contribution." This is the law that stands as the supporting structure of all business and also of our personal well-being.

The paradox is that most people either don't know about this wonderful law, or think that somehow it applies only to the other guy; the way drivers believe we ought to have speed limits—for other drivers. Well, the one predictable thing about most people is that they are consistently wrong.

For example, let's take this law of our rewards in life being in direct proportion to our contribution. Like many great ideas, it's really nothing more than a paraphrasing of a biblical admonition: as ye sow, so shall ye reap.

But, for a moment, look at it this way: laws are good or bad, depending on how we use them. The law of gravity keeps us from flying off into space. But it will also kill us if we step into an elevator shaft. There is nothing wrong with the law of gravity. If we misuse it, there is something wrong with us. Either we are ignorant of the law, or just plain stupid.

Now, let's get back to the law of rewards and contributions. It's like an apothecary scale, the kind with a crossarm on top from which two bowls are suspended. A delicate and honest mechanism. Let us label one of the bowls "Rewards" and the other one "Contributions."

Right here we encounter the problem. Most people concentrate on the bowl marked "Rewards." That is, they want things such as more money, a better home, college for the kids, travel, retirement, etc.—all rewards. But in this hungering for the rewards, they are forgetting the bowl marked "Contributions." In other words, they are concentrating on the wrong bowl. They are like the man who sat in front of the stove and said, "Give me heat, and then I'll give you wood." He could sit there until he froze to death. Stoves don't work that way; neither does life. All we have to do is concentrate on the bowl marked "Contributions"; life and the first law will automatically take care of the rewards! Yet it's a fact that most people have this backward.

But what do we mean by contribution—and to whom do we contribute? You can define contribution as the time and effort you devote to whatever it is you do. And your contribution is to mankind; beginning with the people you directly serve. So you can break it all down to a very simple statement: your rewards will be determined by the way you do your job.

In our exploding economy, if a person isn't happy with his rewards, he should take a good, long look at his contributions. This may seem a hard, ruthless way of looking at things, but remember laws like this are neither good nor bad; it depends on what we do about them.

No one can become rich without enriching others. Anyone who adds to prosperity must prosper in turn.

G. ALEXANDER ORNDORFF

No man who continues to add something to the material, intellectual, and moral well-being of the place in which he lives is left long without proper reward.

BOOKER T. WASHINGTON

Conformity

The Ninety-five Per Cent

If someone asked you, "Do you think you are just like most other people?" you would probably answer, "No." Almost everyone feels he is an unusual individual—different from all others. And it's true; no two human beings are exactly alike. But it's paradoxical that while most people like to think they are different, they try as hard as they can to be alike.

In the past few years you have probably read and heard a lot about the word "conformity."

People are always telling us to be different, to think for ourselves, to be individuals. But do you know why? Well, let me tell you why I think it is an excellent idea to take a good, long look before you start acting and thinking like everybody else.

It seems, from the earliest beginnings of the human race, there have always been two main groups of people. One group is large; it is estimated to consist of about ninety-five per cent of any society. The other is small—about five per cent. It's uncanny how populations seem to insist on dividing into these two groups: the large group of followers, and the small group of leaders. Apparently the people in the ninety-five per cent group never get the word, for they seem to make the same mistakes over and over again and always wind up with the short end of the stick. For example, out of all the young men who start even at age twenty-five, forty years later—by the time they are sixty-five—only five per cent are financially independent. The rest miss the boat. And while money is not "everything," it is an indication of how people handle their lives. Any man, barring a rare catastrophe, can save enough money in a forty-year working career to be financially independent by the time he is sixty-five. But only five per cent know enough at the beginning to plan and save before it is too late. The others will be heard to say, "I wish I had." The big question is, why didn't they?

Further, in this country of ours anyone can get a good education, even if he does not have enough money to go to college. Every town has a public library bursting at the seams with knowledge, perfectly free if you get the books back on time. But do you know how many continue to learn and to develop their minds after they get out of school? That's right—about five per cent! In fact, a well-known educator once said that as far as ninety-five per cent of the people are concerned, all the great books with their priceless stores of knowledge could be taken out in a field and burned, and they would never be missed—only the five per cent would miss them.

This leads one to the conclusion that ninety-five per cent of the people have absolutely no interest in acquiring knowledge. High school and college diplomas are fine, but they are only meant to prepare us for a life of learning so that we can continually improve and move on to new and better achievements.

Most people just go along—acting alike, thinking alike, doing the same things. They feel this must be the safe way. The trouble is that the crowd is all wrong. Traditionally it doesn't know where it is going and, as a result, doesn't get anywhere. If you want to follow in somebody's footsteps, fine; just make sure he, or she, is worthy of emulation. Your friends down the block just may not know where they're going.

Choose always the way that seems best, however rough it may be, and custom will soon render it easy and agreeable.

PYTHAGORAS

There is no tyrant like custom, and no freedom where its edicts are not resisted.

BOVÉE

To follow foolish precedents, and wink with both our eyes, is easier than to think.

COWPER

Work

The Master Word

"The Master Word," written by the great physician, Sir William Osler, is about a word that will work wonders for anyone regardless of age or calling. For man, woman, or child, the master word brings meaning and usefulness to life, new clarity, self-respect, and satisfaction.

As Dr. Osler puts it, "Though little, the master word looms large in meaning. It is the 'open sesame' to every portal, the great equalizer, the philosopher's stone which transmutes all the base metal of humanity into gold. The stupid it will make bright, the bright brilliant, and the brilliant steady.

To youth it brings hope, to the middle-aged confidence, to the aged repose."

Do you know what the master word is? It is WORK!

It has been said that we need reminding as much as we need educating. Human beings have the most perverse tendency to take the best things in life for granted. In fact, a human being has the capacity to take *anything*, no matter how great, for granted—once he becomes used to it. The actor in front of the cameras, the captain of a great ocean liner, the man at the controls of a giant earth-moving machine, the writer, the painter, the mother, all seem to let the charm and excitement of their work fade after a while until it becomes as humdrum to them as brushing their teeth.

William Osler and other great men of the past and present have known the real value of work. Not just its value to those who benefit from it, but its frequently greater value to the person performing it. Men like Osler seem to have the capacity for never taking their work for granted. And because they find it filled with interest and reward, they become great.

I was talking not long ago with a top executive of one of our major oil companies. He had started his career by working as a helper in a service station of the company whose nationwide sales he now directs. Why did he happen to see so much opportunity, adventure and reward hidden in what the average person would consider to be menial, uninteresting work? It makes you wonder how many young men in the same work today are looking beyond the gas tank they are filling or the windshield they are cleaning.

It makes you wonder, too, how a person can take his most precious possessions for granted. How can he allow his loved ones, his home, his health, his abilities, and his work to lose their charm and become dull and dreary? What happens to the excitement of the first days, when his wife, his home and children, his work, were new in his life?

Like the finest silver, these valuable things need regular polishing. They should be kept as bright as they were in the beginning, for once they grow tarnished they may easily be mistaken for things of little or no value.

Even in the meanest sorts of labor, the whole soul of a man is composed into a kind of real harmony the instant he sets himself to work.

CARLYLE

A man is relieved and gay when
he has put his heart into his work
and done his best.

EMERSON

No man is born into the world whose work is not born with him. There is always work, and tools to work with for those who will, and blessed are the horny hands of toil. The busy world shoves angrily aside the man who stands with arms akimbo until occasion tells him what to do, and he who waits to have his task marked out shall die and leave his errand unfulfilled.

JAMES RUSSELL LOWELL

Success

Still the Best Rule

During the past hundred years there have been millions of words written about how to succeed in our personal and business lives. They have told us how to walk, how to smile, how to be enthusiastic. Our magazine, newspaper, radio, and television media tell us how to smell sweet, glow with health, and stay young-looking.

Fine. Each of us wants to sell himself to those who are important to him—his family, his friends, his boss, his co-workers, and his customers. And during many of the past years, I have tried to discover for myself how a person might succeed in life. I have made hundreds of speeches to sales and business groups of all kinds, in just about every state in the Union. From my talks with top-flight businessmen, I have taken enough notes to fill a good-sized garage, all the while trying to draw a composite picture of the really outstanding, successful person. I have talked to old-timers and very young people, fat and skinny people, extroverts and introverts. Incidentally, you might be interested to know that a very large percentage of successful people are introverts. They are miles from being the hearty, bluff, backslapping, hail-fellow-well-met, give-me-that-microphone-I-want-to-say-a-few-words kind of people. Instead, they are just very nice, warm, friendly people, with homes and kids, who decided they wanted more out of life than the average person settles for.

Maybe you will be a little surprised by what my survey uncovered. You might say that I took everything I learned from these people and jammed it into a big wine press, squeezed the whole thing down to its very essence, distilled the essence, and, like Dr. Curie, was left with a radiating substance of incredible power. But, as perhaps you already know, this glowing, wonderful thing I found was not new. In fact, it was incredibly old. Like the sun itself, it has been renewing itself all these centuries and is just as bright and warm and life-giving today as it ever was. When I realized what I had discovered, I knew I had seen it somewhere before; so I pulled down an old, dusty book from my office shelf and finally found the passage that puts it into better words than I or anyone else I know ever could. You can look it up yourself. It is in Matthew 7:12 and it reads: "Therefore all things whatsoever ye would that men should do to you, do ye even so to them: for this is the law and the prophets."

Simple, isn't it? It is so simple, as a matter of fact, it is completely overlooked by the great majority of people. It is the simple, common, everyday things we take for granted that we miss seeing. I remember hearing a man on a train once say, as a fly landed on his sleeve, "They call it the ordinary housefly. You think it's ordinary? Try making one sometime."

Anyway, that is one of the secrets, if you want to call it a secret, of the world's most successful people. They practice one of the world's oldest and best rules—the golden rule.

He that does good to another does also good to himself; not only in the consequence, but in the very act of doing it; for the consciousness of well-doing is an ample reward.

SENECA

Envy

The Revenge of Mediocrity

A person who is superior in any way never escapes envy. People always seem to think in terms of comparison. If a man has a better garden, he is envied by his neighbors; if he gains promotion, he is envied by his fellow workers; if he is able to cope with events so that he lives happily, he is envied by failures. Envy, it has been written, is the one revenge of mediocrity.

And envy is far more rife than it used to be back in the days before democracy. The ancient lines of separation have been erased. In those days, you were either one of the haves or one of the have-nots, and there was nowhere in between. Today, we have reduced the have-nots to such a small minority that the well-being of about ninety per cent of the population is a matter of degree in the ranks of the haves.

The envious man begins by asking, "Why should I not enjoy what others enjoy?" and goes on to demand, "Why should others enjoy what I have not?" Instead of deriving pleasure from what he has, he is pained by the pleasure others receive from what he does not have.

A classic example of this comes to us from ancient Greece. In 1932 an archaeologist unearthed tablets from twenty-four hundred years ago, voting ostracism for a man called Aristides. It seems that Aristides was banished from Athens merely because people hated him for being so much better than themselves. The story is told that as Aristides was walking toward the voting place he was accosted by an illiterate voter who asked him to mark his tablet in favor of banishment. When Aristides asked, "What have you against Aristides? What has he done wrong?" the voter replied, "Nothing, but I'm tired of hearing him called 'the just.' "

Yes, as the proverb says, "Wrath is cruel, and anger is outrageous, but who is able to stand before jealousy?" Probably the only way is to walk along serenely with Aristides, leaving the jealous and the envious to stew in their own juice. It is good to remember what Pliny had to say on the subject: "Envy, wherever it resides, always implies conscious inferiority." That is, the person who envies another is acutely and very painfully conscious of his own inferiority with regard to whatever it is he envies.

We tend to be cruel and vent our rage against those we secretly envy. Eric Hoffer says this is why the Japanese tended to be cruel toward American prisoners of war. They envied the Americans. This was also responsible for the inhuman treatment of the Jews by Hitler and his henchmen. The reason both Japanese and German prisoners were so well treated, as a general rule, by the Allies, is the same, but in reverse: we did not envy them a bit.

The answer is to envy no one. As Horace put it, "The envious man grows lean at the success of his neighbor."

Whoever feels pain in hearing a good character of his neighbor, will feel a pleasure in the reverse. All those who despair to rise in distinction by their virtues, are happy if others can be depressed to a level with themselves.

FRANKLIN

The most certain sign of being born with great qualities is to be born without envy.

LA ROCHEFOUCAULD

Envy's a coal comes hissing hot from hell.

PHILIP BAILEY

Self-knowledge

You're Different

Have you ever found yourself saying, "I wish I were like such-and-such a person"? When we were kids, it was almost impossible to go to a movie without wishing we were the hero. For a while we lived in a vicarious way the dangerous, exciting, or romantic life of make-believe we saw on the screen. But the chances are excellent that we would be completely miserable if it were really possible to trade places with someone else.

One of our most common and worst mistakes is to cover up our own abilities and potentialities by trying to be something we are not. A person could spend a lifetime studying the writings of Hemingway—and never be able to write like Hemingway. The same would apply to acting, singing, painting, or just about anything else. If the person trying to write like Hemingway would write naturally, he would have a much better chance of succeeding. And even more important, he would develop himself as the individual he is meant to be.

As Dr. Ernest Holmes once wrote, "Deep within us . . . within you and me and all people . . . something was planted by Life . . . something that is trying to come forth into fruitage through human endeavor." But it cannot very well come out if we are trying to be something we are not—if we are conforming to a particular group because we think that is the right, or the fashionable, thing to do.

I often wonder, seeing a morning train full of commuters, how many of them are really engrossed in and enriched by what they are doing. All too often they take on the appearance of a herd of cattle on its way to the slaughterhouse. They seem to be playing a part in a play they don't understand, on a stage that is not necessarily of their own choosing. And since they find no real peace or fulfillment in their work, they do their jobs in a perfunctory manner as quickly and easily as possible so that they can quit in the evening and lose themselves in some convenient escape. This is not living; this is really nothing more than waiting for the whole thing to end. This is play-acting.

Finding the real selves we usually keep buried is like prospecting for gold. It is not necessarily easy, but we don't mind the digging so much when we know the gold is really there. It is not like plowing barren ground; riches are there, sometimes way down deep, but somewhere in all of us. And unless a person can find his true self, he will never really know what it means to be fulfilled—to wake up in the morning eager for the day to begin, and to end reluctantly a day which has been filled with interest and challenge—and which has taken some of the best he had to give.

The most interesting journey a person can make is that of discovering himself.

The merit of originality is not novelty, it is sincerity. The believing man is the original man. He believes for himself, not for another.

CARLYLE

Every human being is intended to have a character of his own; to be what no other is, and to do what no other can do.

CHANNING

✡✡

Service

The Chair

And it came to pass that I was looking for a chair last Christmas. I wanted to buy my wife a small telephone chair. I wanted it to be something special—a conversation piece—something that would delight her. It was for the telephone in the butler's pantry which she uses most during the day for her shopping and long visits with her friends. As it was, she had to stand or drag a chair in from the kitchen or dining room.

So, I looked for just the right chair. And I found it. I was delighted, and I knew my wife would be. Yes, it could be delivered in plenty of time for Christmas, I was assured by the personable young salesman.

There was just one thing: I naturally did not want my wife to know she was getting a telephone chair until we opened our presents on Christmas morning. "Will you gift wrap it?" I asked.

The salesman shook his head. "Sorry, we can't wrap it. It will be delivered just as you see it now." But this would take all the fun out of it! "Just put it in an old cardboard box, and I'll gift wrap it myself."

No! the salesman was sorry but it just could not be done. The chair would have to be delivered as is, and Santa Claus would just have to like it—or lump it. In the meantime, the salesman had completed the order and handed it to me for my signature. I shook my head. Sorry, but I would try to find a store with a staff willing to do a little bit more for the customer than just write up an order. I left.

At another very good store, I found another chair that would fill the bill. But the aging, unhappy salesman gave me the same story—no gift wrapping, no box.

Next, I chose the biggest store in town. After two more hours of searching, I found still another chair. Though quite a bit more expensive than the first two, it was an exact reproduction of a famous chair that Napoleon's Josephine used to sit upon.

"I'll take it," I said. Then I paused and silently prayed that I would not again have to continue my odyssey. "Can you gift wrap it for me?"

"We sure can," he said. "We'll find a box that will fit it, wrap it real nice, and your wife will be surprised on Christmas morning."

"Thank you," I said. "You have no idea how much I appreciate that. And since you've been so helpful about it, I saw a chaise longue over there. . . ."

Well, that is the story of the chair. And it is the old story of why people change their buying habits. It is also the reason the biggest store in town is the biggest, and why you would recognize the name if I mentioned it. You might not recognize the names of the other two stores. I won't in the future. They refused me when I needed their help. They didn't earn my money or my future patronage, and so they will get neither. As it is with living creatures, business is a matter of natural selection. The survival of the fittest.

Sow good services; sweet remembrances will grow from them.

MADAME DE STAËL

What do we live for if it is not to make life less difficult to each other.

GEORGE ELIOT

Life is made up not of great sacrifices or

duties, but of little things, in which smiles and kindnesses and small obligations, given habitually, are what win and preserve the heart and secure comfort.

DAVY

280

Enthusiasm

Anticipating the Desirable

One of the more painful aspects of being in business is that, from time to time, you wind up at a convention, find yourself in a crowded hall, and hear someone on the platform shouting his lungs out telling you you have to be enthusiastic. This is as absurd as telling someone he has to be happy, or that he should suddenly laugh or cry. I wonder if these people know what enthusiasm really is. Human beings are enthusiastic because something caused them to feel that way. Enthusiasm is an effect, like happiness or sorrow. Each of these conditions is the result of a cause.

I remember how painfully embarrassing it was for me on one occasion when a nonentity who would not let go of the microphone shouted, "All right—everybody stand up!" Right then I started looking for a convenient exit. There wasn't one. Naturally, everybody stood up, and then he said, "Now I want you to shout at the top of your voices, 'Boy! Am I enthusiastic.' "

This was particularly painful for me because I was among those at the speakers' table, the whole assemblage could see us making fools of ourselves. But we all said it and then sat down quietly squirming with self-consciousness. If there was one emotion I did not feel, it was enthusiasm. The emotions I felt were helpless rage and embarrassment.

I believe a person is enthusiastic because of something he wants and feels he has the ability to bring about. Just as a child is excited about going to the circus, an adult becomes enthusiastic because he anticipates a very desirable event or situation.

People become excited to the extent that they realize they can have the things they want and can live the kind of life they want to live. When a woman sees something in a store window, wants it very much, and knows she can buy it, she is enthusiastic about it. If she feels it is completely beyond her ability to obtain, she will not be enthusiastic, just wistful.

It is the same with men. They become enthusiastic as they recognize their power to achieve their goals. If they feel they are being exhorted to reach goals which are beyond their capabilities or desires, nothing—not all the arm waving and shouting in the world—is going to enthuse them deeply, motivationally.

A man becomes enthused when it dawns on him that he has talents and abilities which are uniquely his own, and that when he decides upon a place in life he would like very much to reach, it is within his capabilities to reach it. Kingsley said, "We act as though comfort and luxury were the chief requirements of life, when all that we need to make us really happy is something to be enthusiastic about." Emerson said, "Every great and commanding movement in the annals of the world is the triumph of enthusiasm."

It is true that nothing great was ever achieved without enthusiasm. But each of us must first find for ourselves the suitable object for such emotion.

No wild enthusiast ever yet could rest until
half mankind were like himself possessed.

COWPER

If we search for the fundamentals which actively motivate us we soon see that they come under four headings: love, money, adventure, and religion. It is to some of these that we always owe that big urge which pushes us onward. Men who squash these impulses and settle down to everyday routine are bound to sink into mediocrity. No man is a complete unit of himself; he needs the contact, the stimulus, and the driving power which is generated by his contact with other men, their ideas, and constantly changing scenes.

EDWARD S. JORDAN

The great accomplishments of man have resulted from the transmission of ideas and enthusiasm.

THOMAS J. WATSON

Persuasion/human relations

A Fable Worth Remembering

As a child you probably read the Aesop's fable about the argument between the sun and the wind as to which was the stronger. The wind said, "Do you see that old man down there? I can make him take his coat off quicker than you can." So the sun went behind a cloud and the wind blew until it was almost a tornado. But the harder it blew, the tighter the old man wrapped his coat around him. Finally, the wind gave up and the sun came out from behind the cloud and smiled kindly upon the old man. Presently, he mopped his brow and pulled off his coat. The sun told the wind that gentleness, warmth, and friendliness are always stronger than force and fury.

Aesop, who gets credit for that fable, was supposed to have lived from about 620 to 560 B.C. Born into slavery, he was said to be ugly and deformed. But he seems to have known more about getting along with people than we now do more than twenty centuries later.

Arguing people, scolding parents, nagging wives, domineering husbands and employers need to realize that people automatically react unfavorably to force, threats, and intimidation. I remember reading about a case where two thousand employees of a trucking concern went on strike for higher wages. Instead of publicly excoriating them, the president of the company praised them. He took an ad in the paper complimenting them on the peaceful way they had put down their tools against what they considered a just grievance.

Finding the pickets idle, he bought them a couple of dozen baseballs, bats, and gloves and invited them to play ball on the company grounds. For those who preferred bowling, he rented a bowling alley. This friendliness on the part of the president did what friendliness always does, it begot friendliness. So the strikers borrowed brooms, shovels, and rubbish carts and began picking up, cleaning up, and generally taking care of the place. Did you ever hear of strikers tidying up the company grounds? Such an event had never been heard of in the long and bitter history of American labor differences. The strike ended with a compromise settlement within a week. It ended without any ill feeling or rancor. The strike was settled—and new respect and admiration were created on both sides.

Benjamin Franklin put it this way: "I early found that when I worked for myself alone, myself alone worked for me. But when I work for others also, others also work for me."

If you have trouble getting along with anyone in your family; your associates at work, or your neighbors, remember that old Aesop fable. The more force you apply, the more you insist upon getting your own way, the less chance you have of winning. You may force a youngster, your wife, or an employee to do what you tell him or her to do, but you have planted the seed of rebellion, and because of this you have really failed in your human relations. Why not try kindliness, warmth, and gentleness; be willing to compromise and see the other person's point of view?

The more I study the world, the more I am convinced of the inability of brute force to create anything durable.

NAPOLEON I

Kindness in ourselves is the honey that blunts the sting of unkindness in another.

LANDOR

Nothing is so strong as gentleness; nothing so gentle as real strength.

FRANCIS DE SALES

Criticism

How to Be Unhappy

I don't know how it affects you, but something that really makes me sad is hearing one human being criticizing another. Whenever I hear a man on the street, or in a restaurant, criticizing his wife . . . or a woman calling down her husband . . . or either one of them giving the same kind of business to a youngster, it distresses me.

Perhaps this is because I have always regarded rancorous criticism as a sign of immaturity. A suggestion given with good humor and love is something else, but I think angry harangues should always be avoided! No two people are alike and because of this no two people can be expected to behave exactly alike. And just because one person holds a certain opinion is no reason another person should think exactly the same way.

Consider, for example, a man and his wife: like everyone else in the world, each of them is a unique individual with strong points and weak points. When one person falls in love with another, it is the total person he loves—the total impression or image. If he compared each feature with the same feature of every other person, he would find others superior in some, inferior in others. He would find no two exactly alike.

The critic is dismayed when he sees that some attribute of the person he loves is not as good or beautiful as it may be in another person. He concentrates on what he comes to think of as a flaw or mark of inferiority. He forgets that no one on earth can be superior to all others in all respects.

That is why real love—well-adjusted and true love—is so wonderful. The total image is so pervasive that the little flaws disappear; they are not noticed or they are loved because they are flaws. That is why the poor deluded person looking for the perfect woman, or perfect man, is looking for something that does not and cannot exist. This is why the real man merely smiles when his wife makes a mistake, or does not rank as high in one particular as another woman might. He understands that he didn't fall in love with perfection.

I think the person who frequently criticizes

others is bound to be unhappy with life and himself. He concentrates on the negative instead of the positive. He doesn't see the sky; he sees the clouds. He doesn't see the miracle of a child; he sees tiny and perfectly natural mistakes. He concentrates on the specks of dust that may be found on any masterpiece and, as a result, goes through life missing the beauty and the wonder of life.

When we see men of worth, we should think of becoming like them; when we see men of a contrary character, we should turn inward and examine ourselves.

CONFUCIUS

Some of the best lessons we ever learn, we learn from our mistakes and failures. The error of the past is the wisdom and success of the future.

TRYON EDWARDS

The legitimate aim of criticism is to direct attention to the excellent. The bad will dig its own grave, and the imperfect may safely be left to that final neglect from which no amount of present undeserved popularity can rescue it.

BOVÉE

Creative thinking

Executive Types

Some time ago I made a speech to the members of a large national organization. These men were executives at or near the top of the companies they represented. I told them that in my opinion none of us thinks *enough; as a rule we let our minds lie dormant until we're confronted with a situation that requires mental effort. I mentioned that even corporation presidents of my acquaintance seldom indulge in serious, concentrated thinking except in times of crises. The fact that they can solve problems and steer their companies safely through crises qualified them as executives and justified their large incomes. But what about all that time they waste between problems? Why not have some sort of systematic daily plan of creative thinking? An intelligent man, as he grows older, works out some program of physical exercise for the proper maintenance of his body—why not a daily program of mental exercise?*

There is a story about a lumber dealer in New York who became an outstanding success in a surprisingly short time. He made millions in the lumber business while his so-called competitors were scrambling around trying to keep up with him. When reporters asked him the secret of his success, he told them that every night he sat quietly all by himself in a darkened room. During this time he simply meditated, trying to imagine how the lumber business would be conducted ten years from then. He would jot down the ideas that came to him and try to put them into effect in his business at once, instead of waiting for the ten years to pass. In this way, while his contemporaries were competing with each other, he was always creating. His secret? Never compete—create! Makes sense, doesn't it?

I try to spend the first hour of each day thinking about our companies and ways in which they can be improved, ways in which we can render better service to our customers and offer it to prospective customers. Right after my clock radio wakes me, and I have listened to the morning news and weather broadcast, I start my hour of thinking. I find that showering, shaving, and dressing are quite compatible with this kind of mental activity. Usually, by the time I get to my office, I have an idea or two to put in the works.

Dr. Frank Braceland, director of the famous Hartford retreat in Connecticut, got a big laugh from an audience of distinguished psychiatrists with this description of the modern executive: "There are four types of executives. First, there's the ulceroidal type, who worries about the problem. Second, there's the thyroidal type, who runs around the problem. Third, there's the adenoidal type, who screams and yells about it, and fourth, there's the hemorrhoidal type, who sits on it and waits for it to clear up."

Every adult is an executive, if not of the company he works for, at least of his own life and his family's. What kind of an executive are you? Are you creating, or are you competing? Why not try each day to do some concentrated, independent thinking about yourself, your life, and the people you serve? I think you will agree with me that *anything*, however good, can be improved.

Thinking is the hardest work there is, which is the probable reason why so few engage in it.

HENRY FORD

There is always a better way.

THOMAS A. EDISON

Living truth is that alone which has its origin

in thinking. Just as a tree bears year after year the same fruit and yet fruit which is each year new, so must all permanently valuable ideas be continually born again in thought.

ALBERT SCHWEITZER

Making decisions

What Would You Tell Your Child?

If you learned this was your last day to live and you were asked to write a formula for living to leave to your children, what would you write? What would you say to give them a wise and true course to follow for the rest of their lives?

They say the best way to learn something is to teach it. If you will write out that formula for living with the idea of passing it along to others, you may find that this will clarify your own thinking and remind you of a lot of simple but important things you can apply in your own life.

Almost all confusion results from indecision. It results from not deciding on a course of action. The minute we choose not to make a decision about something, we put ourselves in the hands of circumstances, or under the control of others who will make a decision. A great American general once said: "Decide; even a wrong decision is better than no decision at all." He meant that if you make a wrong decision, it will usually become apparent, and you can change it. But if you make no decision at all, you will never find out what is right. Another military-type quotation goes like this: "On the beach of hesitation bleach the bones of countless millions who sat down to wait and waiting, died."

So you might want to tell your youngsters to form the habit of making decisions. Most young people in school are not sure what they want to do when they grow up. This is particularly true of boys, and they frequently use this perfectly natural indecision as an excuse. They will say, "Why should I study this (or that) subject if I'm not sure it will be useful in the career I might follow?" Well, I think they should make the decision to get as good a general education as possible. General knowledge will help them make their career decision wisely and when the decision *is* made, they will be bound to have done something toward qualifying for it. They'll have a sound background on which to build the specialty they choose.

We adults excuse our indecision too. We say,

“Why should I knock myself out in the work I’m in, when I don’t like it and don’t intend to spend the rest of my life working at it?” The right decision here is to do the best work of which we are capable, knowing that good work habits are necessary to success in anything, and a high rate of activity, thinking, and studying will help us find the job we want a lot more quickly than just sitting back and hoping for something to happen. Also, by taking this sort of attitude, we are building the kind of references we will need to move into the field we like when we find it.

Carlyle said, “The block of granite which was an obstacle in the pathway of the weak becomes a stepping-stone in the pathway of the strong.” It strikes me that block of granite is often a decision.

The man who insists on seeing with perfect clearness before he decides, never decides. Accept life, and you must accept regret.

FRÉDÉRIC AMIEL

A man without decision can never be said to belong to himself.

JOHN FOSTER

An executive is a man who decides; sometimes he decides right but always he decides.

JOHN H. PATTERSON

Ideals

Concentrate on the Invisible

It has been said many times that if you go through life doing what the great majority of the people do not do, you will probably never make a mistake. This is a generalization, and generalizations are always dangerous. But there is a lot of truth in this one.

For example, most people think the visible things in life are more important than the invisible. They couldn't be more wrong. Opportunity is invisible until we do something about it. A person's dream of what he wants one day to become is invisible. Yet, it is one of the most powerful forces on earth, responsible for all human progress. Love for family and friends is invisible. Faith, belief, courage, patriotism, all are free, all invisible yet vastly more important than visible things. And greatest of all, perhaps, is hope; again invisible. If you think about it, I believe you'll agree that all the valuable things you have acquired are the tangible result of what at one time were hope and faith.

I have in my notebook a quotation the authorship of which unfortunately I cannot ascribe. It goes like this: "There is a thinking stuff from which all things are made, and which, in its original state, permeates, penetrates, and fills the interspaces of the universe.

"A thought, in this substance, produces the very thing imaged by the thought.

"Man can form things in his thought and, by impressing his thought upon formless substance, can cause the thing he thinks about to be created."

Things are really nothing more than thoughts which have become real. As William James once put it, "If you only care enough for a result, you will most certainly achieve it." So if there is something you want very much, think about it and keep thinking about it. Sooner or later you will find a means of achieving it. But, be careful! As Emerson has written: "Be very choosy therefore upon what you set your heart. For if you want it strongly enough, you'll get it."

A surgeon entering the operating room is

only living in reality what was once a dream in his mind. The same is true of all of us from the young wife and mother to the astronaut, to the man who finally gets his golf handicap down to ten. Hope, a strongly held thought, is nothing more than the invisible picture of what will one day be reality.

To quote Leigh Hunt: "There are two worlds, the world that we can measure with line and rule and the world we feel with our hearts and imagination."

In all things it is better to hope than despair.

GOETHE

My country owes me nothing. It gave me as it gives every boy and girl, a chance. It gave me schooling, independence of action, opportunity for service and honor. In no other land could a boy from a country village without inheritance or influential friends look forward with unbounded hope.

HERBERT HOOVER

A fine life is a thought conceived in youth and realized in maturity.

ALFRED DE VIGNY

Opportunity

The World We Look For

Among the writings of Henry David Thoreau I came across this statement: "Many an object is not seen, though it falls within the range of our visual ray, because it does not come within the range of our intellectual ray." In other words, because we are not looking for it or perhaps even capable of looking for it. So in the largest sense the world we see is only the world we look for."

Show two people the same picture and each will see a different scene; each will extract from what he sees that which he happens to be predisposed to look for. Different people looking out of a train window as they pass through the outskirts of a city will see the same thing from entirely different viewpoints. One will see a depressing, rundown neighborhood. Another will see an ideal plant site. Still another might see a marvelous opportunity for a real estate development. The passing scene might give someone else an idea for a story, or a poem, or a song. Another, his face buried in a magazine, will see nothing.

The world presents to each of us every day that which we seek. There is not a neighborhood or area that does not offer abundant opportunity to every person living there. That opportunity is limited only by the viewpoint of the inhabitant.

Some years ago a Wisconsin farmer was stricken with polio and left paralyzed. Flat on his back, unable to farm his land, he was forced to push back his intellectual horizon; he was forced to think creatively, to take mental inventory of his assets and liabilities. Without moving from his bed, he built one of the country's largest and most successful meat-packing companies. Unable to use his hands and feet, he was forced to use his most priceless possession—his mind—and he found it contained all the riches he and his family would ever need. Where before there was only a farm, now there are great industrial plants employing thousands.

I am sure that when his friends and neighbors learned of his affliction they wondered how he would manage to operate his farm and care for his family. He simply looked at the farm with new eyes; he saw what he had failed to see before, even though nothing had changed except his own mobility.

Every one of us lives in a kind of iron lung of his own fashioning. Each one of us has opportunities just as great as that Wisconsin farmer's. But few of us are forced to reach so far into the deep reservoirs of ability within us. And fewer still know the joy and excitement and never-ending interest that can be found in our daily lives when we learn to look at our world as Thoreau looked at his. Surrounded by miracles and limitless opportunity, some people manage to find only boredom and insecurity. As Thoreau said, "We find only the world we look for."

Men seem neither to understand their riches nor their strength. Of the former they believe greater things than they should, of the latter, less.

BACON

I find the great thing in this world is not so much where we stand, as in what direction we are moving.

OLIVER WENDELL HOLMES

The best lightning rod for your protection is your own spine.

EMERSON

Communication

Excess Baggage

One of the principals of a large and successful advertising agency has a hard and fast rule against clichés. A cliché, as you know, is a trite phrase which may have lost its meaning through constant misuse, but which often becomes such a habit that we use it automatically, without thinking about it. I used a cliché in my opening sentence. Did you notice it? I said ". . . . a hard and fast rule." A rule is a rule; the adjectives "hard" and "fast" are probably unnecessary.

They take up valuable time without adding to the message.

The other day I rewrote a two-page letter. By cutting out only the superfluous words, I reduced it to one page consisting of just three paragraphs. Not only was about seventy per cent of the letter unnecessary, but the new version was better. The original letter was fat, unwieldy, and full of clichés—phrases one puts into a letter without even realizing he's doing it.

We have a tendency to speak the same way. Have you ever noticed how often people say, "I mean . . ."? If you simply say what you mean you do not have to tell anyone you're doing it. Another phrase is, "stuff like that," or "in other words," or "like I said." I remember a cabdriver in Philadelphia who would look around after every sentence and ask, "Am I right or wrong?" There is nothing particularly evil about this sort of thing, but it does add a lot of excess baggage to our conversation.

It has been said that the late Ernest Hemingway sometimes spent most of a morning writing a single paragraph. If you read Hemingway, you will notice the effectiveness of a maximum of thought and a minimum of words.

At the site of the battle of Gettysburg in 1863, two men addressed the multitude. One was a celebrated speaker, and he proved it by speaking for two hours. Yet, not a man in twenty thousand can tell you his name—Senator Edward

Everett. The second speaker stood before the crowd less than five minutes, but we all know the Gettysburg Address, and that Abraham Lincoln delivered it. The Gettysburg Address is a simple, powerful message with all the fat trimmed off; seventy-two per cent of this address consists of one syllable words.

The next time you write a letter, particularly a business letter, see if you can do a better job by using simple, strong, hard-working words. Cut out all clichés, such as "with reference to your letter," and perhaps those empty windups. And whenever you write a letter, read it over and ask yourself if you talk like that. If not, don't write like that. And join the crusade against clichés that have lost their meaning or value.

The most powerful words are the simplest one-syllable words. Words such as love . . . joy . . . hope . . . faith . . . home . . . child . . . life . . . death . . . fear . . . kill . . . hate.

Brevity is the best recommendation of speech,
whether in a senator or an orator.

CICERO

A man who uses a great many words
to express his meaning is like a bad marksman
who instead of aiming a single stone at an object
takes up a handful and throws at it in hopes
he may hit.

SAMUEL JOHNSON

The difference between the right word

and the almost right word is the difference between lightning and the lightning bug.

MARK TWAIN

Short words are best and the old words when short are best of all.

WINSTON S. CHURCHILL

Attitude

They're Nicer at the Top

Have you ever noticed that the more successful and important people are the nicer they tend to be? It is all a matter of attitude. You can learn a great deal about a person by studying his attitude. People seem to expect in others the weaknesses and strengths they themselves possess. Consequently the more confident a person is of his own value as a person, the better his attitude toward the world in general.

Big people just naturally treat others well. They are smiling, courteous, and confident. Being happy with themselves, they reflect it; they have nothing to fear. But little people often treat others badly; for they themselves have never really grown up or matured. Something has stunted their inner growth, their confidence in themselves, and since they are not happy within themselves, not confident in their own ability and worth as individuals, they can only see in the world their own reflection. As a result, their treatment of others is a kind of punishment of themselves.

By carefully observing how people—particularly strangers—treat you, you can make a fairly good evaluation of what they think of themselves.

The employees with the best attitude naturally rise to the top of any business. So, the higher you go in any organization, the nicer the people seem to be. Their good attitudes are not the result of their better jobs; their better jobs are a result of their attitudes. Meeting a successful, happy person, people frequently make the mistake of saying, "I'd be happy too, if I had what he's got." It's perhaps natural to think his attitude is the result of his success, but just the reverse is true.

William James wrote: "The greatest discovery of my generation is that people can alter their lives by altering their attitudes of mind." Each of us attracts the kind of life he, as an individual, represents. That is, before a person can achieve something, he must become the kind of person this "something" would naturally belong to.

(If you can visualize how you would act if you had everything you wanted, begin to act that way now and make that kind of attitude a habit. The attitude must precede the accomplishment.) Most people have this backward and, as a result, wonder why they never quite make the grade. If you want to be happy, act like a happy person. One day you will wake up to find happiness has come to you, and you will never quite know when the acting stopped and the reality began. That is why Lincoln's comment that people are about as happy as they make up their minds to be is true. As a great teacher once said, "A good mental attitude is even better than mental ability." Your attitude tells the world what you expect from life. And you will receive exactly that, no more, no less.

Mind is the master power that moulds and
makes, and man is mind, and evermore he takes
the tool of thought, and shaping what he wills,
brings forth a thousand joys, a thousand ills:
He thinks in secret and it comes to pass
environment is but his looking-glass.

JAMES ALLEN

All our actions take their hue from the complexion of the heart, as landscapes do their variety from light.

W. T. BACON

Nothing can stop the man with the right mental attitude from achieving his goal; nothing on earth can help the man with the wrong mental attitude.

W. W. ZIEGE

Self-control

Temper, Temper

Of all the creatures on earth, man is among the youngest. It really has not been a very long time since we were primitive savages. And while we now are able to annihilate each other with atomic weapons rather than stone axes, most of us still have difficulty maintaining a calm, smooth, civilized disposition in some of the circumstances which confront us.

Yet the highest type of human being is the one who manages to control the more antisocial of his primitive urges. Take anger, for example. There is no one more disliked or more to be pitied than the person who cannot control his temper. I know, because for years I had the problem. I paid for it, too, in many ways—and it is not worth it!

A mother with staring eyes, flushed face, and clawing hands, screaming in anger at her child, is a ghastly sight. And there's a sad correlation here; the wider she opens her mouth to shout in anger, the narrower is her intelligence.

Men who go through life making their families and friends walk on eggs for fear of their infamous and insane rages are small men, really. They have never matured. And being proud of a hot and violent temper is about as intelligent as being proud of dishonesty or stupidity.

Young ladies who smile and warn their young men that they have a quick temper are saying that they are immature and that they will make embarrassing and unsatisfactory wives—and miserable mothers. And millions of them go on to do just that.

The bad-tempered bully, whether in school or in later life, is universally despised. More than that, he is sick. He is proclaiming ignorantly to the world that he has never grown up, and that if everything does not go his way, he will turn back the clock of human progress and act like a prehistoric savage with no more intelligence than an ululating gibbon.

As James Allen wrote: "The strong, calm man is always loved and revered. He is like a shade-giving tree in a thirsty land or a sheltering rock in a storm." The same is true of a woman who is well developed enough emotionally to radiate the calming influence of a peaceful mind and heart. These people see through the effects to the causes of things. Instead of screaming at their children, which does no good at all, they take a more intelligent approach. They do not *expect* children to act like grown-ups. If another adult does something they do not like, they understand why: they will more than likely feel sorry for the person rather than angry.

I cannot imagine anyone wanting to be feared rather than loved. We love people who have developed mature tranquility, and we like to be around them. They have the *capacity* for indignation, and they are most effective in changing a situation that they know is wrong. In fact, if you are looking for a fight, and want to pick on somebody, steer clear of the calm, self-possessed individual. He will make you look like a blithering idiot. And, if you would grow into a person people love and respect, develop a calm attitude and a tranquil heart.

A tart temper never mellows with age, and
a sharp tongue is the only edged tool that grows
keener with constant use.

WASHINGTON IRVING

Self-reverence, self-knowledge, self-control,
those three alone lead life to sovereign power.

TENNYSON

Don't permit yourself to show temper. Always

remember that if you are right you can afford to keep your temper, and if you are wrong you cannot afford to lose it.

J. J. REYNOLDS

Security

We Need to Be Needed

Every man, woman, and child wants security, but only a small and fortunate few ever attain it.

We know, for example, that a job does not in itself offer security. We often find two men working for the same company and in the same department; one of the men is secure in his job—the other is not. And this is true of people in almost any situation, including the players on the high school football team or the members of a family.

Let me give you one of my ideas about security and see if you agree. I think the people who have the greatest security are those who are doing the most to secure the situation in which they find themselves.

The security of a person working for a company depends upon the security of the company itself. Therefore, those individuals who make the greatest contribution to the continuing success of the company are the most secure; those who do the least are least secure. The boy who contributes most to the success of his football team has the best chance of getting in and staying in the game. So we can say, then, that a person is secure to the extent that he is needed. And he will be needed to the extent that he has developed the capability of doing successfully the things that need to be done.

The areas in which he should develop himself most are those in which he is most depended upon. A married woman, then, should concentrate on her home, her family, and her social relationships. A man should concentrate on his work *and* his family and social relationships. Most of us accept the fact that we must remain insecure in all but a few situations. I would feel insecure in a professional golf or bridge tournament. I enjoy playing both games for fun and relaxation, but I don't have the skills and experience to compete with the professionals in those fields. And I cannot fly a passenger jet, or command a ship at sea, or even fix my car if it stops running.

But we can all develop the security we need for the situations we are regularly called upon to meet and have freely chosen. We can do it by learning to do what we do as well as it can possibly be done. We may not achieve this ideal, but in striving toward it we will become secure as persons.

Security, then, lies not outside us but inside. The wonderful thing about developing this kind of security is that we take it with us wherever we go and can never lose it. And like everything good in life, it is there to be earned if we seriously want it.

In all the affairs of life let it be your great care not to hurt your mind or offend your judgment. This rule, if observed carefully in all your deportment, will be a mighty security to you in your undertakings.

EPICTETUS

The confidence which we have in ourselves gives birth to much of that which we have in others.

LA ROCHEFOUCAULD

Trust men and they will be true to you; treat them greatly and they will show themselves great.

EMERSON

Self-discipline

Oh No You Wouldn't!

A fine woman pianist once gave a performance for a large group of women. Afterward, over coffee, a woman gushed to the virtuoso, "I'd give anything *to play as you do."*

The woman who had given the concert took a sip of her coffee and fixed the red-faced, slightly perspiring matron with a cold gaze. Then she said, "Oh no you wouldn't!"

A hush fell over the group, coffee cups stopped on their ways to and from saucers, and the perspiring matron squirmed in sudden embarrassment. Looking about her she repeated, but in a softer voice, her original statement, "I would, too, *give anything to play the piano as you do."*

The female virtuoso continued to sip her coffee and shake her head. "No, you wouldn't," she repeated. "If you would, you could *play as well as I do, possibly better, possibly a little worse. You'd give anything to play as I do except time . . . except the one thing it takes. You wouldn't sit and practice, hour after hour, day after day, year after year." Then she flashed a warm smile, "Please understand," she said, "I'm not criticizing. I'm just telling you that when you say you'd give* anything *to play as I do, you really don't mean it. You really don't mean it at all."*

In the pause that followed, a napkin falling to the rug would have rattled the windows. The women looked at each other and then back at their coffee cups. They realized that this woman had spoken the truth. They would like to have her talent now, fully matured and developed; but as for putting in the twenty years of unremitting toil that went into the fashioning of it—no, that was a different matter. Soon, the light conversation was resumed and the incident was glossed over, but not forgotten.

People are forever saying, "I'd give anything . . ."; but the fact remains that they don't, they give very little, often nothing, to do the things they say they would give anything to do.

Those who envy the star performers in any field should realize that across the entire galaxy of achievement the stars are those who did not idly wish for success. They gave their dedication, their singleness of purpose, their days and nights, weeks, months, and years to an unceasing struggle for greater proficiency. And when the talent they have so painstakingly cultivated for so long begins to bloom, others, who had the same time, the same opportunity, the same freedom, come up to them and say, "I'd give anything to be able to do what you're doing, to have the things you have." But as the lady pianist said: "I'm just telling you that when you say you'd give anything to play as I do, you really don't mean it. You really don't mean it at all."

Why not become what you dream of? Each of us has the time and the opportunity. If we say we do not, we are perhaps kidding ourselves. With enough effort and perseverance everyone can become great at *something*.

Sometimes it seems there are far too many spectators in the game of life and not enough players. Maybe we are so busy watching the world and everyone else that we forget we have a world of our own to win.

People do not lack strength, they lack will.

VICTOR HUGO

Every man stamps his value on himself. The price we challenge for ourselves is given us by others. Man is made great or little by his own will.

SCHILLER

There is no genius in life like the genius of energy and industry.

MITCHELL

322

Courtesy

Important Words

Two of the most important, most neglected words in the English language are "thank you." Most people who fail to say "thank you" don't mean to be rude. But that is the impression they convey. They just forget—or haven't been raised properly—or are too self-conscious—to put these two important words into use.

When we do someone a favor, we needn't expect him to fall on his knees, but we do expect to be thanked. A favor accepted without any sign of appreciation is like an unpaid bill for goods received.

Some people develop a little trick to remind an offender of his lack of courtesy. Whenever a cashier in a restaurant fails to say, "Thank you," they say, "You're welcome." Whenever they hold a door open for a stranger who passes through without saying, "Thank you," they say, "You're welcome." The offender usually looks embarrassed, even startled. But at least he has been reminded of his omission.

A lot of people need reminding.

A friend of mine once held open the door of a Boston department store just to test people's reaction. He told me that fifty people passed through the open door before one of them said, "Thank you."

Words are free: it doesn't cost anything to be polite. Yet people are surprisingly quick to complain and slow to express appreciation. The boor who bawls out a waitress because his food doesn't please him so often takes a good meal for granted without complimenting the chef. A radio commentator can do a good job for years without one letter of congratulation, but let him mispronounce one word and the station switchboard lights up like a Christmas tree. A letter of congratulation always brightens the day for anyone. But for every complimentary letter received by writers and editors, there are dozens of venomous diatribes from critical cranks.

Big people are courteous to a fault; it is only the little people of the world who are not. And none of us is too busy or too important to express thoughtfulness and genuine appreciation, to say, "Thank you."

Bulwer wrote: "What a rare gift is that of manners! How difficult to define: how much more difficult to impart! Better for a man to possess them than to have wealth, beauty, or talent. . . ."

Well, I wouldn't perhaps go that far. But I would say, "Thank you," wherever and whenever I could. And I hope you would too.

We cannot always oblige, but we can always speak obligingly.

VOLTAIRE

Manners are more important than laws. Upon them in a great measure laws depend. The law can touch us here and there, now and then. Manners are what vex or soothe, corrupt or purify, exalt or debase, barbarize or refine, by a constant, steady uniform insensible operation like that of the air we breathe. They give their whole form and color to our lives.

BURKE

Using time wisely

A Twenty-Year Head Start

When the vice-president in charge of sales of a large Western company retired, everybody in the sales force assumed his job would go to the senior salesman—let's call him Tom—who had been with the firm twenty-five years. And the one man most certain that job would go to Tom, was Tom himself. In fact, he had been counting on it since first he discovered his boss was planning to retire.

For at least two years, Tom had been talking about it to his wife and children, their friends and neighbors, and his fellow salesmen. The job meant a substantial raise in pay, and Tom and his wife had been planning things they could do with the extra income. For about three months, they had been poring over travel folders outlining a trip to the Orient.

So when Tom was called into the president's office on the morning following the retirement party for the former vice-president, he was wearing his best suit and a smile to match. What he had no way of knowing was that his boss was facing the kind of situation that makes company presidents worth every penny of their excellent incomes. He had an Armageddon on his hands.

After the president had winced through the cheerful "good morning" and dapper appearance of his senior salesman, he looked him straight in the eye and said, "Tom, I have to tell you that the executive committee has awarded the position of vice-president in charge of sales to Bill Smith."

There followed a vast, deep silence. They could have been in a diving bell at the bottom of the Marianas Trench. After two or three hoarse, croaking starts, Tom finally managed to protest. "But Bill has been with the company only *five* years. I've been here twenty-five!"

Well, enough of that. Facing the other men of the sales force and going home to face the family was agony for Tom. But in the weeks and months that followed, it finally dawned on him that he had confused seniority with accomplishment. Tom didn't really have twenty-five years' experience with his company; he had *one* year's experience repeated twenty-five times!

Bill Smith, in just five years, had far outdistanced Tom in growth, knowledge, and ability. While Tom was putting in time, Bill was putting in everything he had, and now a young man, with his head crammed with detailed information on every phase of the company's operations, with great plans for the future and five years of outstanding sales production behind him, Bill Smith found himself vice-president in charge of sales. The gentlemen of the executive committee had made a wise decision. They were interested in the growth of the company, not Tom's planned trip to the Orient. What's more, they now have young Bill Smith earmarked for the presidency of the whole company. When that happens, if Tom wakes up, he might get that vice-presidency after all.

Sad story? Sad for whom? Tom could have had that job. He had a twenty-year head start. [As Albert Einstein discovered, time is relative. Its only value to us depends upon what we do while it is passing. Time means nothing at all to a stone or a fence post, but it can mean a great deal to a man.]

A man that is young in years may be old in hours, if he has lost no time.

BACON

Improve your opportunities. Every hour lost in youth is a chance of future misfortune.

NAPOLEON I

If time be of all things the most precious, wasting time must be the greatest prodigality, since lost time is never found again; and what we call time enough always proves little enough. Let us then be up and doing, and doing to the purpose; so by diligence shall we do more with less perplexity.

FRANKLIN

Gratitude

The Luckiest People on Earth

Do you know who the luckiest people on earth are? To my way of thinking, they are those who have developed an almost constant sense of gratitude.

A person who is not conscious of living, of happiness, and of all the things living embodies, might just as well not be living at all. This is perhaps what Socrates meant when he said the unexamined life is not worth living.

The luckiest people are those who are grateful for their work and grateful that they can do their work and do it well. They are grateful for their children and their wives and husbands. They never take them for granted; never permit them to lose their love, interest, and charm. They are grateful for their lives, their health, their friends, and their opportunities. And they have about them an aura of good cheer and well-being.

They are not Pollyannas. They are aware of the ugly and the sordid things that go on about them but they do not permit themselves to be dismayed. When trouble comes their way, they seem to know that it is only temporary and they tackle trouble like a linebacker cutting through to nail a quarterback for a ten-yard loss. And when the trouble has been taken care of, they dust off their hands and go charging out into life again.

If I had to pick out the one quality that makes these people different from the millions who live defensive, insecure lives I would say it is their sense of gratitude. They are so grateful for all the good things they don't have time for preoccupation with the unpleasant.

Children are experts at this. I once watched a little boy—he must have been about two—at play. Raising himself up quickly, he banged his head on a table. He had hit his head so hard that it made him sit down, and there he sat for a minute, rubbing the spot, with his face puckered up and a couple of big tears in his eyes. Suddenly, though, he got to his feet and away he went, still rubbing his head, but with his mind on more interesting things. There was nothing he could do to alter the fact that he had a new lump on his head, but he was not going to sit in a corner and spend the rest of his day worrying about it.

The grateful people never lose this happy faculty. They expect the best from life and, as we all do, they get what they expect ninety-five per cent of the time. They take their lumps and move out again, looking for things that are more fun and more rewarding. They wake up in the morning grateful that they are alive and go to bed the same way at night. They seem to have an acute consciousness, an awareness that they are living every second of their lives. They enjoy their food and their sleep, their loved ones and their work.

We all know people like this. And we can learn from them. And perhaps the best way to begin is to develop a sense of gratitude.

Happy the man who can endure the highest and lowest fortune.

SENECA

Sometimes the brightest day hath a cloud, and summer evermore succeeds barren winter with its wrathful nipping cold. So cares and joys abound as seasons flee.

SHAKESPEARE

Persistence

Nothing Can Replace It

People often wonder how certain individuals seem to accomplish so much during their lives. Those who achieve unusual success are often regarded as different, geniuses, or lucky; or they are believed to have some magic formula. But the fact is that one thing typifies the successful person: persistence.

There is a quotation: "Nothing in the world can take the place of persistence. Talent will not, nothing is more common. Genius will not, unrewarded genius is almost a proverb. Education will not, the world is full of educated derelicts. Persistence and determination alone are omnipotent."

Just as the person who stays with the study of medicine will become a doctor some day, any person who makes up his mind what he wants and has the determination to stay with it will most certainly obtain it. [The trouble with most people is that they don't know what they want. They first try one thing and then another, or perhaps they just mark time, waiting for some unknown opportunity to come along. If they would only choose a goal and pursue it with determination and persistence, they could relax in the certain knowledge that while it might take a long time, one day they would assuredly reach it.]

Persistence makes dreams come true. If a person persists long enough, he will become qualified for that which he seeks. Talent will help, as will genius and education; the more you have for you, the better. But the fact remains that a person can be quite short in the talent and education departments and still get where he wants to go—if only he has *chosen* his destination.

I have long believed that the reason people do not accomplish more is that they do not know what causes success. They think it is difficult and complicated and involves many years of study, financial backing and some kind of wizardry. As a result, they do nothing at all.

Persistence sounds easy, but it is not easy at all. All kinds of obstacles present themselves, some of them so serious, or seemingly so, that you think there is no way on earth to get around them. At times like these, the person without enough persistence finds it easy to rationalize abandoning his goal. His excuses may sound fine and convincing, even to himself, but they are still excuses —nothing more.

Someone once wrote to me that he had always wanted to write a book, but for years had been too busy. Now that he was retired and had plenty of time, he said he was too upset to write.
334 *Persistence* Finding excuses for not doing something is easy; finding the persistence to do it is something else again.

Perfection is attained by slow degrees; it requires the hand of time.

VOLTAIRE

An enterprise, when fairly once begun, should not be left till all that ought is won.

Shakespeare

No road is too long to the man who advances deliberately and without undue haste, and no honors are too distant for the man who prepares himself for them with patience.

BRUYÈRE

Consider the postage stamp, my son. Its usefulness consists in its ability to stick to one thing until it gets there.

ANONYMOUS